USING
ICT
in
GEOGRAPHY

**FRED MARTIN AND
TIM REA**
with
Keith Grimwade

Fred Martin is a tutor on the Bath Spa University College PGCE 'Geography with ICT' course.

Tim Rea is head of the humanities Faculty at St George School in Bristol

Keith Grimwade is the Cambridgeshire LEA adviser for humanities.

Orders: please contact Bookpoint Ltd, 39 Milton Park, Abingdon, Oxon OX14 4TD. Telephone: (44) 01235 400414, Fax: (44) 01235 400454. Lines are open from 9.00 – 6.00, Monday to Saturday, with a 24 hour message answering service. Email address: orders@bookpoint.co.uk

British Library Cataloguing in Publication Data
A catalogue record for this title is available from The British Library

ISBN 0 340 77166 6

First published 1999
Impression number   10 9 8 7 6 5 4 3
Year   2005 2004 2003 2002 2001 2000

Designed and Typeset by D&J Hunter Book Design and Production Services, Shortlands, Kent.
Printed in Great Britain for Hodder & Stoughton, a division of Hodder Headline Plc,
338 Euston Road, London NW1 3BH by Hobbs the Printers Ltd.

Contents

Introduction

DfEE Circular 4/98 Annex B; Initial Teacher Training Curriculum for the Use of Information and Communications Technology in Subject Teaching

http://www.open.gov. uk/dfee/circular/0498. htm

Teachers Annex A1 (England, Northern Ireland and Wales) The use of ITC in Subject Teaching, Expected Outcomes for Teachers in England, Northern Ireland and Wales

Web address at www.teach-tta.gov.uk/ ict/index.htm

Aim

*T*he aim of these resources is to help teachers to make use of some of the different applications of Information and Communications Technology (ICT) for the teaching and learning of geography in a secondary school. Although ICT is generally defined as including all types of electronic methods of communication, the emphasis in these resources is on the uses of computer hardware, software and peripherals. This focus may help teachers to interpret and apply the standards that are set out in the DfEE Annex B document on the use of ICT. These are the standards that apply to all geography and all other trainee teachers from September 1998. The same standards are also to apply to the training of all currently serving teachers, irrespective of subject specialism and phase.

Level

Most of the techniques involve little more than using relatively simple sets of keyboard commands. A few use hardware and software that is a little more specialist, but are nevertheless, still relatively easy to operate. All the ideas are written from the perspective of the geography teachers as user, rather than as an ICT specialist. The more technical aspects of ICT such as setting up hardware and operating systems for running software, can best be left to ICT technicians and other specialist ICT staff.

Taking Decisions

It is never the intention to claim that ICT is either the only or the most effective way to carry out any particular learning task. Teachers and pupils need to develop the critical framework to make these kinds of decisions in the context of their own school. It is important however, to have the right information so that informed choices can be made.

Structure

The contents are organised in a way that tries to reflect how ICT can be used for work in geography. After an opening section on planning the use of ICT, most sections then concentrate on one of a limited number of applications of ICT, such as on data handling and the Internet. Some however, such as on location of weather and mapping, aim to stress the idea that effective use of ICT can often be achieved by using several different applications, moving between them for particular tasks and to access different types of resource. The extent to which working in this ICT-rich environment can replace or complement using hard copy work with pupils, is a question that individual teachers need to consider.

The sequence of chapters

It is difficult to devise a single sequence in which to learn how to make use of ICT in geography. Some basics are certainly essential, such as a knowledge of file management and word processing. Other applications however, can be learnt in almost any order. There is therefore, no need to use the chapters in the order in which they have been presented. Working with the Internet for example, is no more easy or difficult than using a spreadsheet or drawing program. Although some skills are common between them, learning how to use them is not entirely linear.

Keys to learning ICT

Ten basic keys to learning about the use of ICT may be of use. These are items derived from personal experiences rather than from established research. They may however, be of some use to a teacher who is starting to develop their ICT skills.

- Make sure you understand the basics of *file management*, using whatever mental images you need to understand what the computer is doing to the data you input to it. Although the common language of 'files', 'documents' and 'folders' may be familiar, their use in computer jargon also needs to be understood.

- Appreciate the ways and extent to which different applications have features *in common* with each other. Toolbars in a word processor and spreadsheet have much in common, as well as having some differences. Learn the techniques to copy and paste data and information between applications and to access data in other files.

- Understand the principles of how each type of application works and the order in which it needs things to be done. Understand for example, that you need to highlight text or click on an object *before* you choose an instruction that will apply to it, not the other way round.

- Work *from a particular outcome* that you want to achieve for your own subject purposes, then learn about the functions you need in a program to accomplish it. Leave functions that appear to be more difficult or of no immediate use until you do need them. This approach creates gaps to learning, but the advantages of learning in context are likely to outweigh the problems.

- When asking for advice from ICT-literate colleagues, first *describe the end result* you want to achieve. Let them work out which application you need to use and the functions you need to use, then ask them to show you what to do. Do not allow anyone else to touch the mouse while you are learning. Listen to instructions, but do it yourself.

- Learn how to make the most of the hardware and software you already have.

- Understand that what is ultimately important is not the knowledge of how an individual item of software functions, but to develop *the creativity* to use both subject-specific and generic software for your own teaching purposes.

- Be positive in your learning and try to *avoid blaming yourself* if something goes wrong. A problem may be caused by a hardware or software fault, the software may be badly written to make it unintelligible, or there may be several other causes both explicable and sometimes even to an 'expert', inexplicable. You may have done something wrong, but it is only one of several options. Frustration comes more from blaming yourself than blaming a machine.

- Don't worry if you forget how to carry out a function. This is inevitable. You can relearn how to do it later. But make sure to *practice functions* that you think you will immediately be able to use.
- Don't worry that some pupils know more about hardware and software than you do. Be happy to learn from them. Besides, they may know how it works but you *know what to do with it*.

The sample activities

Two sample activities are provided in each chapter. These aim to show how a range of applications of ICT can be incorporated into normal teaching and learning activities in ways that can:
- add qualitative value to the geographical content
- take advantage of the capabilities of ICT, e.g. speed, capacity, range, provisionality, interactivity, etc. (see Annex B document to DfEE Circular 4/98).
- provide an alternative or complementary teaching and learning strategy
- can help with structure, organisation and enhance the appearance of students' work.

Access to ICT

The activities assume that there is access to the widest range of hardware and software. It is recognised that this assumption is unrealistic in many schools. They should however, provide ideas as to what is possible to do, perhaps with modification.

Age range for activities

An age range for which the activities are most suitable is provided on the chart. This is based both on the ICT skills needed and the nature of their geographical content. Teachers will make their own decisions as to what is appropriate for their students.

Disc data

The activities with some supporting data are provided on a floppy disc that accompanies the pack. The material is mainly written by using generic software such as a word processor and spreadsheet. This should enable teachers to:
- modify the wording of activities
- edit, add or delete the sample data
- run the activities on a network or download to a stand-alone PC.

The nature and extent of this resource is limited by:
- the limited storage capacity of a floppy disc (without using a zip facility)
- the limitations of the software to handle compressed file formats for images (most files are written using Word 6 and use Paintbrush in Windows 3.1 or Paint in Windows '95).

There is considerable further potential for teachers to create their own files of activities by making use of the functions and tools in these generic programs.

Working with ITC; the activities

Chapter	Activity 1 – title	Activity1 – ICT	Activity 2 – title	Activity 2 – ICT
Ch 2; Working with words	The growth and function of settlements KS3	◆ Research using CD-ROMs ◆ Create a wordprocessed document	Volcanic landscapes KS3	◆ Use a spell checker ◆ Editing a wordprocessed document
Ch 3; Using data	Population change KS3	◆ Enter and sort data in a spreadsheet ◆ Process data in a spreadsheet ◆ Draw graphs using a spreadsheet	Industrial location KS4	◆ Enter data in a spreadsheet ◆ Modelling spreadsheet data by changing variables
Ch 4; Photographs on screen	Landform processes KS4	◆ Acquire, then import a photo into a drawing program ◆ Annotate and manipulate a photo ◆ Create a wordprocessed document	Local area study KS3	◆ Use a digital camera and photo processing program ◆ Annotate a photo ◆ Use a word processor ◆ Communicate using Email
Ch 5; Finding out	Levels of economic development Post 16	◆ Research statistics and photos using CD-ROMs ◆ Import clip art to a drawing program ◆ Create a wordprocessed document	Natural disasters KS4	◆ Research using CD-ROMs ◆ Create a wordprocessed document
Ch 6; Drawing programs	Forest in Europe KS3	◆ Draw or import a map into a drawing program ◆ Draw a colour-coded map ◆ Create a wordprocessed document	Environmental issues KS4	◆ Draw, import or scan a base map into a drawing program ◆ Add map data and annotation to the base map ◆ Create a wordprocessed document
Ch 7; The weather report	Weather disaster research KS4	◆ Research information using the Internet, CD-ROMs and other ICT technologies ◆ Draw a map using a CD-atlas and drawing program ◆ Create a wordprocessed document	Tropical climate Post 16	◆ Research data using CD-ROMs ◆ Enter raw data into a spreadsheet ◆ Draw graphs in a spreadsheet ◆ Create a wordprocessed document
Ch 8; Maps and mapping	An environmental enquiry KS3	◆ Sort text in a word processor ◆ Draw or import a base map into a mapping or drawing program ◆ Annotate the map with quantitative symbols ◆ Create a wordprocessed document	River field study Post 16	◆ Draw an accurate map using a mapping program ◆ Use a digital camera ◆ Use a multi-media authoring program to present information
Ch 9; Using the Internet	Weather forecasting KS3	◆ Use the Internet for weather data data and satellite imagery ◆ Enter data on a table in a word processor	Study skills KS4	◆ Use an Internet website ◆ Make notes in a word processor

1 ICT in the classroom

1.1 Planning for ICT

*P*lanning the use of ICT, especially the use of computers, is essential if the technology is to play an effective part in teaching and learning. Although most of this pack is devoted to practical ideas and techniques, none of these can be applied without developing a pedagogy to make use of them in the classroom. Although some of the issues are not new and relate equally to other type of technology and resources, the use of computers is bringing a range of questions and issues that need to be addressed in order to make the best use of them.

Three broad aspects of ICT are outlined in this section.
- Planning ICT in geography
- Hardware and software
- Staff training.

1.2 Planning ICT in geography

An understanding of the potential benefits of using ICT in geography should make it clear that it can not be regarded as an optional type of resource. As a key resource for teaching and learning, there needs to be a detailed strategy to implement ICT that takes the following into account;
- writing Schemes of Work
- teaching and learning styles
- the role of ICT in achieving differentiation
- gender issues
- access to ICT facilities
- the growth in home computers

In all of these matters, it is only possible to provide some ideas for guidance about the issues that are likely to arise. Details of how these issues can be resolved are still being worked out in the context of individual schools.

An outline to illustrate the use of ICT in studying a country.

Notes

In this module, pupils make the choice of country to be studied.

- The outline only lists ICT resources to be used, though texts, reference books, video and other resources would also be used. The style of working could be either as individual work or as groupwork.

- Organisation of the work would need to take account of access to hardware, software and the competence to use ICT.

- Assessment can take account of Level Descriptions in both geography and in IT.

Module title

The economically developing world; country study

Year 9

Module length; 7 weeks with 2 lessons each week at 60 minutes length

Key questions	ICT activities
How is an economically developing country defined?	◆ Use a CD-atlas with bank of socio-economic data ◆ Use a spreadsheet to enter data; rank data to define the least economically developed Choose an EDC to study.
What are the country's main physical features and what effects do they have on people?	◆ CD-atlas or encyclopedia for maps of physical features including climate and natural vegetation ◆ Satellite imagery to identify environments ◆ Printouts of maps and import to drawing program to create base maps ◆ CD-newspaper to research natural disasters ◆ Use a word processor to write an account of people-environment relationships
What are the country's population characteristics and pattern of settlement?	◆ CD-atlas with bank of statistics ◆ Use a spreadsheet to graph population characteristics ◆ Use a mapping or drawing program to map settlements and settlement patterns
What are the main economic activities and how are they being developed?	◆ Satellite imagery to identify land use ◆ Country-CD if available e.g. (India or Kenya) ◆ CD-photobase and use scanner to copy photos to illustrate economic activities ◆ Use of a drawing program to illustrate and label economic activities
What similarities and differences are there between two of the country's regions? What are the main environmental issues?	◆ CD-encyclopedia, CD-photobase and Internet for details of similarities and differences ◆ Create a document to describe and illustrate the similarities and differences ◆ Internet web sites to research issues and viewpoints CD-newspapers for details and comment ◆ Create document using photos, maps and diagrams imported into a word processor.
What links and relationships does the county have with other countries?	◆ Internet web-sites to identify patterns of trade, tourism, aid and other international links ◆ CD-encyclopedia and CD-atlas to crosscheck Internet data.

1.2.1 Writing Schemes of Work

A Scheme of Work provides a planning tool in which the role of ICT can be clearly stated.

- The use of ICT already forms part of the NC Orders for Geography, though the exact nature of its contribution is left for each department to work out.

- Irrespective of the NC Orders for Geography, individual pieces of software and hardware can be identified as key resources to help develop most aspects of work in geography. For some topics, the use of ICT can be one of a number of other resources. Work on settlements for example, may use text books, videos and maps, as well as the optional use of one or more applications of ICT. At the other extreme, a whole module can be based on the use of ICT with one program or piece of hardware such as a mapping program or a weather station as the main resource.

- In many schools, there is an expectation that every department plays some part in teaching the requirements of the NC Orders for IT. To do this means that work using ICT in geography and in other subjects needs to be related both to the subject Orders, as well as to the Programmes of Study and Level Descriptions in the NC Orders for IT. The effect of this requirement means that there needs to be at least a minimum contribution to working with ICT from every department and therefore from every teacher. This is the only way to ensure that all pupils have equal opportunities to achieve their potential in ICT. For subjects, this requirement can be taught through the use of generic software such as word processing and drawing programs, by using more specialist subject-specific programs, or both.

- The use of ICT now provides pupils with independent access to a much wider range of information and ideas than has previously been possible, at least with the same ease of access. This ought to raise questions about the extent of prescription with regard to factual content that needs to be written into a Scheme of Work. There are many opportunities for pupils themselves to make choices over what to study. They need no longer be confined to studying the one country or city that happens to be the case study in a course text book. Instead, more independent work can be done, though still within an overall structure of key ideas and questions provided by a teacher. There are certainly some advantages in giving greater choice to pupils, though writing and managing a more content-free Scheme of Work is clearly not without its problems.

- One aspect of ICT planning in a cross-curricular manner involves devising a coherent approach to the development of basic ICT skills for the pupils. Some of this work is likely to be done during KS1 and KS2, but this may be on a different type of computer or some degree of upgrading may be needed, for example between different versions of the Windows operating system. These kind of basic skills involve procedures such as using a scroll bar or Enter key, opening files or moving between programs. A progressive sequence of skills needs to be devised and time allocated to teach them, either with or without a subject context. Some part of geography teaching time may need to be devoted to doing this, perhaps at the expense of doing something else. Faced with this responsibility, geography teachers may need to make hard choices between coverage of their own subject, and spending time developing these key ICT skills.

1.2.2 Teaching and learning styles

The use of ICT is itself a particular style of teaching and learning. There are variations in the ways that this can be done.

- Work in a computer room where there are many computers, tends to be done either individually or in pairs, depending on class size and the number of computers. Teachers need to be aware of potential software problems in advance so that each individual or pair does not require attention at the same time and so that more occasional problems can be quickly resolved.

- Work using a single stand-alone computer in a classroom is potentially more complex to organize, especially in the context of a secondary school where pupils for a minority subject such as geography are likely to be seen for a short length of time with long intervals between lessons. A long term plan is needed to ensure that all pupils have an equal entitlement to ICT resources. This may involve using a different program but with a parallel application during a different topic. Using a spreadsheet for example, could be done during several different modules rather than making sure that each pupil does identical work in each module. Careful record keeping is needed to make sure that opportunity is achieved for all. This applies to pupils who both welcome opportunities to make use of ICT, and those who are rather more reticent.

- Working with ICT should not be regarded either as a reward for those who have completed other work or as a discrete and unrelated activity.

- Care needs to be taken that contact with the teacher is maintained and that learning is not entirely devolved to a learning program. Although computers can create some element of motivation and novelty in the short term, teaching and learning remains a process that requires a high level of interaction between teacher and pupil and also between the pupils themselves.

- Pupils are able to work at a pace that is appropriate to their own abilities when they have a greater degree of control over their resources. This is different from a situation where the teacher dictates the pace of work, sometimes literally, when talking through a set of slides or when pupils are watching a video. Pupils setting their own pace of work is of course, not without its problems.

- When choice of factual content is more open to pupil choice, the role of the teacher may become one of helping the pupil to interpret the material, devising learning structures and also at times, in helping to resolve problems in running the software.

1.2.3. ICT and differentiation

ICT is one of many strategies that can play a part in achieving differentiation in a number of ways.

- Many programs make use of different types of stimulus material. Multi-media programs for example, will typically contain not only text and still images, but also sound, animation and video. This range can help provide access to the resources for a wide range of pupils, some of whom may find visual material more accessible than material presented only as text.

- The style of work using ICT may appeal more to the ways in which some pupils learn than to others. The interactive facilities on some programs can produce the illusion of a kinestethic style of learning. A simple illustration of this is the way in which a computer 'cut and paste' function can simulate using a scissors and glue. Fortunately, the computer version does not have the same risk of mess or danger.

- A balance between lessons that involve using ICT and other learning styles helps give greatest access to learning for the greatest number of pupils.

- Work produced by the teacher on a word processor and put onto a screen can easily be adapted to different levels. Doing this also avoids the need to print short runs of differentiated sheets. The idea of working at different levels is something to which pupils who are accustomed to computer games can easily relate. The challenge in these games is to move on to the more complex levels.

- The amount of resources that pupils access can differ, ranging for example, from a limited set of photos through to accessing a much larger photo bank. Opportunities to research further

The IT Orders; characteristics of performance*

◆ Communicating information; e.g. using word processors, desktop publishing, presentation programs, multi-media authoring

◆ Handling Information; researching information using CD-ROMs, recording and saving data on spreadsheets and databases, testing hypotheses

◆ Controlling and measuring; using instructions to control equipment, taking readings using sensors

◆ Modelling; testing ideas by changing variables, simulations and models

* The text and the heading above are being changed for the revised IT orders

details and occasionally to go in different directions are made easier by access to CD-ROMs and the Internet.

■ Many less able pupils have problems of communicating in written English to the extent that it acts as a brake on demonstrating their level of achievement in geography. Words typed on screen then manipulated and checked for spelling can help overcome this problem, though it is unlikely to completely resolve it. There are similar advantages for pupils whose cartographic skills are limited through lack of skills or lack of equipment.

1.2.4 Assessment issues

Assessment of geography when using ICT, and also of pupils' achievement in ICT as defined in the NC Orders for IT, raises several issues.

■ The assessment of ICT at KS3 may be organized on a whole school basis rather than through a separate IT department. This puts a responsibility on the geography teachers to be aware of the Programmes of Study and the Level Descriptions in IT as well as in geography.

■ The process of compiling a portfolio of work for assessment is more complex when examples of work using ICT may be needed to illustrate achievement in more than one subject.

■ There are practical problems in identifying who has actually produced work in ICT when pupils often work in pairs. Identical pieces of work can be printed out with no clues as to the nature or extent of each person's contribution.

■ Questions about the conditions under which work outside school has been done may need to be raised. There may be little other than writing style to help identify the work's author.

■ In geography, teachers may need to redefine the criteria used to assess geographical skills with respect to map drawing and other graphics. A comparison for example, may need to be made between a freehand sketch map from one pupil compared to one

drawn using clip art and a drawing program from another. Allocating marks for spelling and other aspects of written English on GCSE coursework is a problem when pupils can check their work both for grammar and spelling, even accepting that these facilities must be used with care.

■ Geography teachers may find that there are occasions when the outcomes of work using ICT needs to have a different emphasis because of the need to provide an assessment for the IT Orders. To do this, two different marking criteria may be needed. However, since a level should not be given to any one piece of work, at least it should be possible to avoid giving two different levels to the same item.

■ Work done on a computer is as prone to being lost as hard copy work in a file or exercise book. Floppy discs can be corrupted and work can be wiped out. At worst, a problem to a network server can wipe out every pupil's work. The importance of keeping a backup is impossible to exaggerate. Fortunately, there are several ways in which this can be done ranging from making a copy of each file on a different floppy disc, to whole school systems that make backups at the end of each day.

1.2.5 Gender issues

Any generalisation in relation to gender and styles of learning is bound to be problematic. Nevertheless, some broad comments can be made about ways in which gender relates to teaching and learning with ICT.

■ The word 'technology' in Information and Communications Technology' is perhaps unfortunate. It may unfairly carry connotations that can be misinterpreted as making it a largely male preserve. The addition of 'communications' may do something to change this perception. The fact that it is not usually the technology that is important, but how to apply the technology is what needs to be stressed.

■ Many of the commercial computer games most commonly available may relate more to the interests of boys than to girls. This may have the effect of giving boys an initial advantage and a greater interest in the use of ICT. Fortunately, geography software does not seem to have this kind of male bias.

- Specialist ICT teachers are more likely to be male than female. This however is little more than historic accident in that ICT has often developed from the needs of maths and science where there have been more male teachers. It is up to all teachers in a school to demonstrate that there is no reason for this gender link to be made.

- Boys and girls may have different perceptions as to the potential value of ICT in their future careers. This will inevitably affect their perception of its relevance to them.

- Some boys show a marked preference to working in a more individual manner. For those boys, working alone on a computer can be more enjoyable than working together as a group. Other aspects of the style of working with a computer may also appeal to them.

- A drawing program or word processor can help create equality with regard to the overall appearance and neatness of a pupil's work. This also applies to standards of written English where at certain ages, boys appear to be performing at a level below that of girls.

In spite of these generalisations, it is worth remembering that differences between pupils other than gender, are likely to have an even greater effect on how they work with ICT. What is more important is that teachers try to identify indvidual strengths and learning preferences so that ICT can play a part in raising achievement for all.

1.2.6 Access to computers

Access to computers is one of the greatest problems facing geography teachers in their use of ICT with pupils. The issue is difficult to resolve as it involves using what is usually a whole school resource for which there are many competing demands.

- The greatest barrier to use by a geography department can be the existence of a separate GCSE in IT or where core ICT skills must be taught as part of a GNVQ course. Although this kind of work can help create a pool of pupils who are highly ICT-literate, it can lead to increased problems of access to ICT facilities for other subjects.

- A way to avoid a similar problem at KS3 is to ensure that there is a full commitment to teaching all aspects of the IT Orders from all subjects. This includes the need to provide credible assessments for achievement in IT. One implication of this approach is that there is a need for a high level of IT training for all staff. Another is the need for a high level of co-ordination in matters such as assessment and room booking.

- Frictions of distance can create a different kind of access problem. Accident of location can put the geography department in a different building to that of the ICT resources. This affects ease of room booking, the use of lesson time and separating the ICT work from other geography resources.

- Use of a single or small number of computers in the geography classroom, whether operating as stand-alone stations or linked to a network, does provide constant access. It also sets a climate in which the use of computers is seen as a fully integrated part of learning. The problems of managing adequate and equal access to stand-alone computers however, are considerable.

- One option is to move towards a system of small clusters of computers, possibly in combination with other learning resources. These can be located in different parts of the school, each serving a limited number of subjects. This approach creates problems of supervision, technician help, finding appropriate locations and the installation of cables to network programs. It also involves a move towards more resourced-based learning styles. This however, may be an option that is worth considering.

Key words

- front end; the screen design and system that gives access to programs

- hardware; the equipment

- PC; personal computer

- peripherals; items of equipment that can be linked to a computer such as a digital camera

- platform; the type of computer operating system

- stand-alone computer; a computer that is not linked to any other computer

- work station; the hardware a user needs to enter and access software

- applications; the different ways to apply software

- CD-ROM; a compact disc on which data and information is stored for access but not for new data to be entered

- CD; a compact disc

- floppy disc; a disc on which work can be saved

- generic software; programs to carry out general tasks such as word processing

- hard drive; space in the computer where files can be saved

- program; an item of software

1.2.7 Home computers

The increase in home computers has been dramatic in recent years. In some schools, a high percentage of students either have their own computer at home, or have easy access to one. The rate and pattern of ownership however is patchy. For the teacher, there are some implications of this with regard to planning lessons.

- In some respects, a computer at home is no different from the extent to which pupils have always had different degrees of access to resources such as books or foreign travel. There is no completely effective way of compensating for these differences and it is equally unlikely that equal access to a computer can be achieved.

- A problem however, is that access to a computer may become an essential part of a pupil's work in geography, or may give considerable advantages to those who do. Without equal access, it is hard to set homework that involves using a computer. Schemes of Work that involve the extensive use of ICT can therefore disenfranchise some pupils. Yet with local area networks and use of an Intranet, home and school computers are already being linked.

Some aspects of learning may increasingly be denied to those who do not have this kind of access.

- One scenario resulting from unequal access is that two different kinds of learning in geography could develop. One would make maximum use of ICT in areas such as GIS, data handling and information retrieval. The other could remain tied to more traditional methods and resources. It is a matter of debate as to which approach would give the better geography.

- Greater access to computers in the school is one way to achieve greater equality.   One approach is to run school computer 'clubs' in the early morning, lunch time and after school. Even this however, brings staffing and organisational problems. Unless carefully monitored, the end result may be little more than pupils who can play computer games. Games however, may create openings to develop other ICT skills, interests and applications.

- Although reference in this section has been solely to computers, the same ideas also apply to the availability of periherals such as digital cameras, scanners, and digital video.

1.3 Hardware and software

The geography teacher does not need a technical understanding of ICT hardware or systems. There are however, some items that require a basic level of understanding for the ICT user. These relate to;

- platforms
- working with software
- networking.

1.3.1 PCs and other platforms

There are several different platforms in current use of which the PC (IBM compatible Personal Computer), Acorn such as the Archimedes and Mac. such as the Apple are the most common in UK secondary schools. At home, many children may be more familiar with Amiga computers. The same kind of applications apply to each type of platform, though

there are some details that are different in how the software and hardware is used. Some items of software are written in different versions to be run on different platforms. For others, the software may be specific to one platform.

- The choice of platform is seldom if ever made by the geography department. As a potentially major user however, it is a decision that ought to involve the geography department. For

Applications of ICT (computers)

◆ control; to give commands to a computer so that different actions can follow

◆ databases; programs to store, access and process complex data

◆ desk top publishing; to design pages of text and illustrations

◆ drawing programs; drawing pictures and diagrams

◆ Email; a way to send messages using a computer

◆ image processing; to capture and edit photos and other images

◆ Internet; access to information kept on computers all over the world

◆ modelling; to feed data into a computer that changes variables so that hypotheses can be tested and results predicted

◆ multi-media authoring; using text, sound, pictures and video to present information

◆ presentation programs; to present key ideas to an audience

◆ spreadsheets; to put data and text onto a sheet for ease of reference and for calculations

◆ word processing; the ability to type text then edit it

a geography department, the availability of software and peripherals that are relevant to geography is likely to be the major consideration over which platform to choose. Other departments in a school may have different criteria for their choice, for example if their main requirement is for the platform to handle sound or graphics.

■ Technical details of how these platforms operate need not be the concern of the geography user. Whichever platform is used, it is the job of the IT co-ordinator or technician to make sure that use is as easy as possible. Doing this means designing a 'front end' screen that gives easy access to programs. The geography teacher must be able to articulate needs, preferably making use of appropriate ICT jargon. The inability to ask the right questions at the right time can unfortunately lead to the provision of inappropriate solutions.

1.3.2. Working with software

The word software describes the various programs that create the range of different types of applications of ICT. The software can be bought as a floppy disc, on compact disc (CD), or it may come as a program already installed on a computer's own hard drive.

■ A useful distinction can be made between generic software and software that has subject content. Generic software includes programs for word processing, working with data and for drawing. They come with no subject content. Subject-specific software gives content on topics, usually as CD-ROMs, (compact discs with a read only memory). The most effective uses of ICT involves using both types of software. This can be done either by working with both types at the same time, for example, when cutting and pasting data from one to create a document in another.

■ A mistake is to think of ICT use as based solely on a limited number of subject-specific programs. Although individual programs may have excellent

content, it is the development of transferable ICT skills that will help create the most effective ICT users. The generic programs also offer enormous possibilities for subject use.

■ Software needs to be evaluated before it is purchased. Some items are made available for inspection, but not every publisher offers this facility. Reviews of software are available in journals such as 'Teaching Geography'. The BECTA (formerly NCET) website is another invaluable source of evaluations. Remember however, that CD reviews as with book reviews, may tell as much about the reviewer as about what is being reviewed.

```
Key Organisations

BECTA
British Educational
Communications and Technology

National Grid for Learning (NGFL)
```

■ Software evaluation has to be in the context of each school's hardware and the requirements of each department's Scheme of Work. The purchase cost of the software is a major factor, though this can be complex to work out on account of the different types of licences. The cost of a program to run on a stand-alone computer for example, can be very different from the cost of running the same program across a network.

■ Sharing software, both generic and subject-specific, is one way to spread the high cost of some software. A multi-media authoring program for example, should be seen as a whole school resource. Some content-rich programs however, may also have cross-subject applications such as between geography and science. This is when a co-ordinated and co-operative approach is needed.

■ Whatever software is bought, it is likely that a considerable amount of additional work may need to be done to make it of use with pupils. Although some programs contain pupil activities, many do not. Besides, even built-in activities may need to be modified.

Key words

- LCD; a liquid crystal display unit, used on top of a powerful overhead projector to project a computer screen image on a wall screen

- network; a way of linking work stations so that the same software can be addressed and saved from each station

- password; a code word used by an individual computer user who is working on a network

- projection system; a projector to display a computer screen image on a wall screen

- user area; a part of the computer's space for accessing and saving work that can only be used by the user after entering a password

1.3.3 ICT in the classroom

One key question about planning ICT use concerns whether it is to be on a single stand-alone computer in the classroom, or if it can be run on a network in a computer room. Each mehod involves different teaching and learning styles, as well as technical questions about the software and hardware. As always, different costs are also involved in the choice.

- Running programs on a network means that the same program can be used by each pupil at the same time. This gives gives better access to all, but often runs into problems of booking pupils into a computer suite. There may also be technical limitations in running the program effectively across a network.

- In general, full multi-media programs are difficult to run on networks. This is in spite of publishers' claims to have this capability. Some run text and still images, but can crash when an animation, sound or video is involved. Some CDs run slowly when used on several stations at once, while others that handle more simple graphics may have no problems. The problem usually lies with the hardware, especially with the type of cabling, rather than with the software. This problem can be resolved but it involves technical and cost issues that a geography department can not resolve on its own.

- As a general rule, the more simple the program, the easier it is to run it on a network. A simple program that can be networked may for this reason alone, be of greater use and value than a more complex one that can not.

- An alternative use of a multi-media CD is to use it as an electronic blackboard by linking it to an LCD panel or computer projector system. Both types of projector puts the computer screen image onto a wall screen. A third option is to use a large 'touch screen' projection system. Using a CD in this way is certainly effective but projection hardware is still expensive, not easily moved, and the time to set it up between lessons may not be available.

- A network is one way in which pupils can have access to their own user space. An individual password allows each pupil to save their work on the network's main hard drive. Saving to a stand-alone computer involves either using floppy discs or saving on the computer's hard drive. The latter is problematic in that the amount of hard drive space is unlikely to cater for what may be needed.

- The technical aspects of networking are best left to an ICT technician though as with other aspects of ICT, the geographer's special requirements may need to be explained to see if they can be accommodated.

1.4 Staff training

Many teachers do not feel either competent or confident in their ICT abilities. A few have a reaction to ICT that is little short of hostile. Others have taken ICT in their stride both for their general professional work and for work in their subject. A government initiative is now in place to ensure that all teachers improve their ICT skills. Several strategies are available to help improve staff ICT skills in a department.

- A Scheme of Work with a commitment to using ICT may be needed to encourage all staff in a department to become involved.

- An understanding of people's apprehensions is essential to help those who are most reticent. Training needs to be done in a way that is clear and uses plain language, rather than in a way that assumes too much and moves too quickly.

- INSET time needs to be allocated for ICT training in order both to create the time to learn in manageable stages, and to stress the importance of such training.

- The benefits of using ICT need to be clearly demonstrated. Teachers should be encouraged to visit ICT lessons that are taught by others who are more competent.

- Staff need to share in the production of resources that are needed to accompany the use of ICT.
- Few if any ICT 'experts' have a complete understanding of every type of application and every aspect of teaching and learning with ICT. The most productive type of training is one in which everyone is encouraged to share what they know, as well as learning new skills. Even the most simple ideas may not have occured to someone else.

1.5 Conclusions

ICT has the potential to bring about large scale changes to teaching and learning in schools, but in particular in geography. Becoming ICT-literate has moved from being an option to an essential part of the job of every teacher. This involves developing a knowledge of the language of ICT, the skills in using ICT and the ability to make effective use of ICT in the classroom. Much of the pedagogy of working with ICT has yet to be worked out.

Changes in software and hardware have been rapid in recent years. Further changes can be expected. There have also been and continue to be, changes to the curriculum and to the expectations of what teachers can do. Some aspects of these changes are related, for example the way in which increased access to hardware and software is generating as well as responding to changes. What is more important is that none of these changes can be ignored.

Little if any of the ideas presented in these resources, are not already being done in schools. If anything, the ideas can be criticised for not being sufficiently comprehensive. It is an aspect of teaching and learning that is likely to need regular updating.

2 Working with words

2.1 Introduction

*W*ordprocessing gives the user the ability to type text, save it, then access it so that it can be changed in almost any way imaginable. It is one of the main ways in which a computer can be used to communicate information. The skills needed for word processing form the basis of the skills needed for many other types of work with ICT. These skills involve both basic keyboard skills and the ability to make use of the various word processing functions.

Word processors

- The most basic word processor on a PC that uses the Windows platform is called **Write**. The Write program is found in the Accessories group of programs.

- **Word** is the word processor in the MSOffice suite of programs. There are different versions of Word, depending on its age.

- Other word processor programs are also available.

- A 'bundle' is the word used to describe all software loaded on the computer's hard drive or that is bought on CD as part of the purchase price.

2.1.1 Transferable skills

A basic word processor comes as part of the bundle of software installed on most computers. More advanced word processors can be bought and installed onto a computer's hard drive. Word processors vary in their functions and complexity but all, especially those that work in Windows, have enough in common to make the skills to use them transferable from one to the other.

2.1.2 Changing features

Word processing plays a large part in a range of other types of applications. Desk top publishing, multi-media authoring, Email and creating presentations for example, all make use of basic word processing skills. Although each of these applications have their differences, two changes have taken place as the software has developed.

- The different applications have become more interchangeable, for example, by

including a wider range of functions in each type of program. A good word processing program is now able to perform many of the same tasks as a desk top publishing program. This gives greater choice as to which type of application to use for the same basic task.

- Specialist programs now include a much greater range of functions. Word processor and other types of applications now contain far more functions than are needed by most users. A problem can be that more time is then spent in using the additional presentation functions than is justified by the nature of the task.

Although some of these functions can be of use, learning the basics can usually be accomplished without becoming confused by them.

2.1.3 Transfering text

Five other features of word processing are also worth knowing.

- Text written using one word processor

Move between programs in Windows 3.1

- Click on the minimise icon in the top right of the screen

- A program icon appears at the bottom of the screen.

- Run the other program you want to use.

- To go back to the first program, first minimise the second program.

- Then double click on the first program icon.

Move between programs on Acorn computers

◆ Select the program from the icon bar.

Quick move between programs in Windows (PCs)

◆ An easy way to move between programs is to hold down the Alt key, then tap the Tab key.

◆ In turn, at each tap of the Tab key, the name of each program that is opened apears in a small window in the middle of the screen.

◆ Release the keys when the program you want is identified.

Move between programs using windows (PCs)

◆ Two or more programs can be kept on the screen at once by reducing the size of the windows in which they are seen. This is done by using an icon in the top right of the screen to partly minimise the window, then by clicking on and dragging the window's surrounding box to make it smaller. A program is reactivated by clicking on any visible part of its window.

Move between programs in Windows '95 and later versions

◆ Click on the minus icon in the top right of the screen

◆ The program then appears as a labeled bar near the bottom of the screen.

◆ Run the second program you want to use.

◆ To restore the first program, click once on its name in the bar.

can be loaded into a different version of the same program. Doing this however, is only possible when a program is able to recognise that another version or program exists. An early version of Word for example, will not know that a later version exists. A later version such as Word 7, will of course know that Word 2 or Word 6 exists.

■ A document written in one word processor such as Write, can be read into a different type of word processor such as Word 7. Again, this can only be done if the original program is recognised. It may also be the case that some of the formatting is lost when a more advanced program is translated down to a more basic one.

■ Text from one application can be copied and pasted into another, for example from a wordprocessed document to Email.

■ Text can be saved in a basic form as *Text Only* in the *Save As* option. This makes it available to the widest range of other word processors.

■ Special software allows documents created on one platform to be read on another platform. Maklink Plus is an example of a program which allows documents to be moved between an Apple Mackintosh and a PC.

2.1.4 Managing files

Using wordprocessed files involves some knowledge of how each platform and operating systems works. This involves some knowledge of;

■ basic functions such as saving, editing, printing and formatting

■ file formats

■ file management in directories or folders.

Although these are key generic skills in using a computer, they are best learnt in the context of one's own computer.

The main requirement for file management is to have a clear structure worked out as to the headings and sub-headings you think will be most suitable for the files you need to create and save. Creating names of directories, e.g. in Windows 3.1 and Acorn, or folders e.g. in Windows 95 and Apple, involves nothing other than choosing an option to create a directory or folder then giving it a name.

2.1.5 Applications using text

There are five main types of applications that make extensive use of text. Most have additional features such as the use of pictures and sound. All of these have the potential for use in geography.

■ Word processing

■ Desk top publishing (DTP)

■ Presentation programs

■ Multi-media authoring

■ Special purpose programs

Key words

◆ document; a single page or set of pages to make one document with its own file name

◆ font; the type of letters, including style, size and colour

◆ style; the different types of lettering, e.g. Times New Roman, Arial etc.

Moving text in Word

◆ Hold down the left button on the mouse and drag the pointer over the text to be moved.

◆ Release the mouse button when the text is highlighted. The pointer over the highlighted text now changes to an arrow.

◆ While the pointer is over the highlighted text as an arrow, click the left mouse button and hold it down. A small rectangle appears beneath the pointer.

◆ Keeping the button down, drag the text to a new position.

◆ Release the button when it is in place.

2.2 Word processing

The key features of word processing can be listed as;
- writing and editing text
- spelling, grammar and the meaning of words
- designing layouts
- copy or cut and paste between programs
- drawing tools

2.2.1 Text

One advantage of a word processor over handwritten text is that it allows ideas to remain fluid until the final document is ready to be read or printed. Changes can be made easily and without a loss in the quality of its appearance.

- Text size and style can be changed to suit a particular audience. Different fonts are likely to be effective with different pupils. Emphasis can be achieved by using bold, italic or underlining. Text can also be written in different colours.
- Words can be reordered and replaced. Whole paragraphs and pages can be moved around to create alternative structures to a flow of ideas.
- A word count can be instantly given, either for the whole document or for sections of it.
- Text can be sorted and put into alphabetical order.
- Individual words can be found using a search function. Words can also be replaced either individually or on each occasion that they appear.
- Statistics about the text can be provided such as dates when typed, the time it has taken and other organisational data.
- Text can be highlighted by giving it borders of different styles.

2.2.2 Spelling, grammar and meaning

Most word processors can check for spelling and grammar, as well as to look up word meanings and give alternatives.

- The ability to check spelling is useful for identifying some errors. A spell check however, identifies words that have a correct spelling but in a different context. It is easy for example, to mistype 'he' instead of 'the', or to type 'to' instead of 'too'. Pupils need to be made aware of the limitations of a spell check as well as its advantages.
- A dictionary or Thesaurus is part of some programs. These can help to explain words or to choose a more appropriate word.
- A check on English grammar can be made, though it is often acceptable to break some of the stricter rules with no adverse effect on the meaning.
- A reading age for the text can be obtained, for example in MS Word. These need some interpretation but can give clues about the likely level of text difficulty.

Counts:	
Words	471
Characters	2,172
Paragraphs	15
Sentences	39
Averages:	
Sentences per Paragraph	2.6
Words per Sentence	12.1
Characters per Word	4.4
Readability:	
Passive Sentences	38%
Flesch Reading Ease	77.4
Flesch-Kincaid Grade Level	5.4
Coleman-Liau Grade Level	8.3
Bormuth Grade Level	9.2

Statistics in MS Word word processor

2.2.3 Layouts

The appearance of a document can help make it either accessible or impenetrable.

■ Layouts can be chosen from a range of templates that have been designed for different purposes. A layout can also be created to suit more individual needs.

■ Choosing the number of columns is one way to improve readability. A two column layout with relatively short line lengths is likely to be easier to read than one that uses the full page width.

■ A layout that is vertical (portrait) or horizontal (landscape) can be chosen to suit the shape and size of illustrations or text to be included. A world map for example, may need a landscape layout to fit it to its largest size.

2.2.4 Copy, cut and paste

Other pieces of text or art work can be copied or cut and pasted into a word processor.

■ Some word processors have their own bank of clip art that can easily be imported into a document.

■ Tables and graphs can be imported from spreadsheets and data bases. A spreadsheet is a function already built into the MS Word word processor.

■ Photos, maps and diagrams can be imported from drawing programs.

2.2.5 Drawing tools

Some word processor programs have their own bank of drawing tools. These can be used to draw different shapes and lines in any colour. These are drawn as a separate

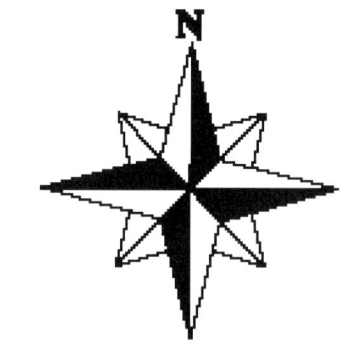

Compass from the Word clip art

An outline of Australia; Powerpoint clip art

Image of a city; Powerpoint clip art

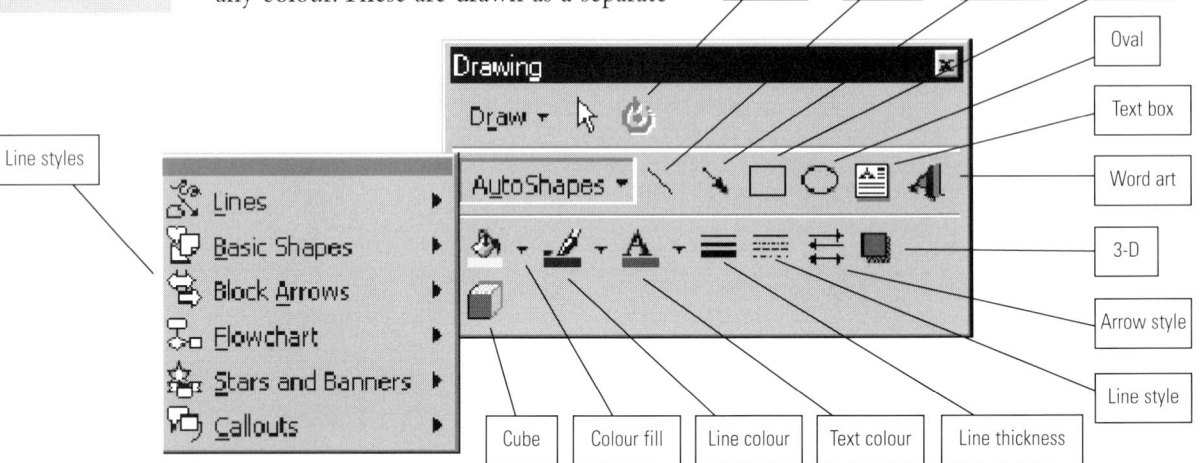

Drawing tools in Word

layer over the basic document. Further details of drawing tools is given in Chapter 6 on Drawing programs.

Text boxes can be put on the page in any position. A user can add more text in the box by clicking inside it then typing.

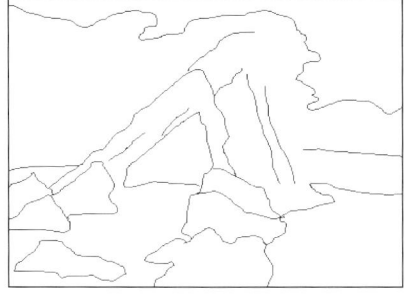

A line drawing using Word's drawing tools

Word 7

Word 7 is the word processor that is part of the MSOffice '97 suite of programs. It has all the functions of Word 6 and earlier versions of Word. It also has some additional features that can be used to create resources for geography.

Some types of resources can be printed as hard copy. Others however, can be designed to be used entirely on-screen. The latter is where several of the additional features of Word 7 can be most effectively used.

Although Word 7 is not a DTP program, it does have many of the functions of a DTP program and can be used as a substitute if one is not available.

♦ Photos and other illustrations as JPEG or other compressed file formats can be imported into a Word 7 document. Only bitmap (bmp.) images can be imported into Word 6 documents. The JPEG images take up considerably less disc space and are a common way that photos are saved for other purposes.

♦ Hyperlinks can be created using Word 7. This sets up direct links either to a different place in the same document, or to a different file. The link can also go directly to a particular place in a different file. This allows the user to create resources with choices as to where to look for information or activities. Hyperlinks can also be created that take the user directly to an Internet or Intranet web site.

♦ Word art can be used to make text such as titles look more attractive.

♦ Text can be saved in html format. This makes it easy to use in Internet or Intranet web authoring.

♦ A document map in Word 7 gives the option to see the headings and sub-headings contained in the whole document, then to move directly to the section required.

♦ Text can be animated, e.g. by making it flash, blink or to be contained in an animated frame.

♦ Sound can be imported and run.

An editable feature

◆ An editable feature is one that can be changed.

◆ Changes are made by clicking on the feature with the left mouse button. This highlights the feature by putting a box around it. There are 8 small squares called handles along the edges of the box.

◆ By clicking exactly on a handle, the size and shape of the box can be changed. The outline can be dragged to a new position by clicking on the outline box away from the handles.

◆ Text or other drawings inside the feature can also be changed.

◆ A frame can be created and pictures or clip art imported into the frame.

2.3 Desk top publishing

A desk top publishing (DTP) program is a means of creating documents where layout is important and where there is likely to be a need to include photos or art work. There are few additional skills to those needed for word processing and other generic applications, other than learning how to use the DTP software.

■ A design for the page is created using boxes that are dragged and positioned as required. Standard layouts are available as templates or stationery templates you can reuse. Wizards or assistants may give step by step guidance to help you create the design you want.

■ Text and illustrations are put into the boxes. Text can be changed in the same way as with word processing.

■ Each box is an editable feature, in the same way as a text box can be edited in the Word word processor. The box can be moved to a new position, its shape can be changed and the text in it can be changed.

■ Special features can make the appearance more attractive, for example by making text wrap around illustrations. Text can be manipulated to give more interesting visual effects such as in circles or in different shapes.

■ Photos and other illustrations can usually be handled in a greater variety of formats than in the older word processor programs. Some of these formats allow photos to be saved in a way that takes less disc space. The photos can be processed in another program before being imported, or cut to fit when in the DTP program.

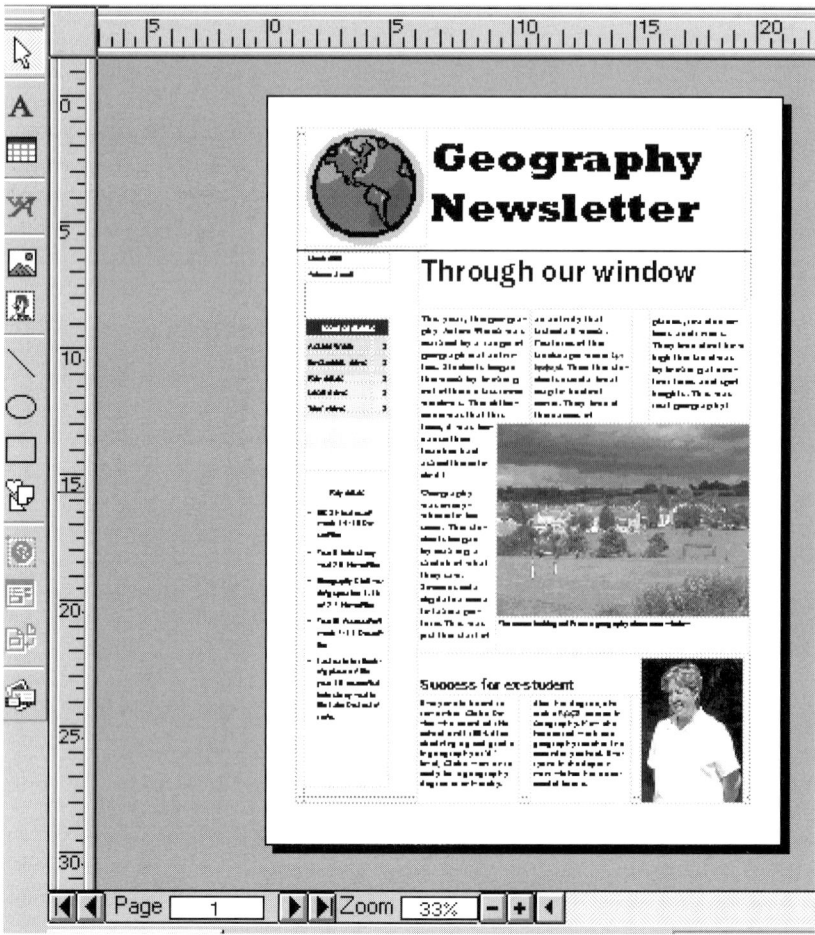

Using the MS Publisher '98 desk top publishing program to create a newsletter

Key words

♦ presentation; using the computer to present text and illustrations to an audience

♦ slide; one screen of a presentation

♦ transition; the way a slide changes from one to another, e.g. as blinds, dissolving or other patterns

♦ build; the way that text appears on the slide, e.g. to fly across the screen from a direction, to dissolve etc..

♦ viewer; part of the presentation program that allows a presentation to be run

2.4 Presentation programs

Some programs are designed to be used as part of a formal presentation in front of an audience. The Powerpoint program in MSOffice is one example of this kind of application.

2.4.1 Writing a presentation

Once the content is worked out, writing the presentation is mainly a matter of following screen instructions. These allow choices to be made as to the final appearance of the presentation.

■ Different templates are provided as background for the text. These include different colours, designs and layouts.

■ Text can be typed in any size, style and colours as with a word processing program.

■ A sequence of individual slides is built up to form the presentation. New slides can be added, deleted or put into a different order. The presentation however, runs in

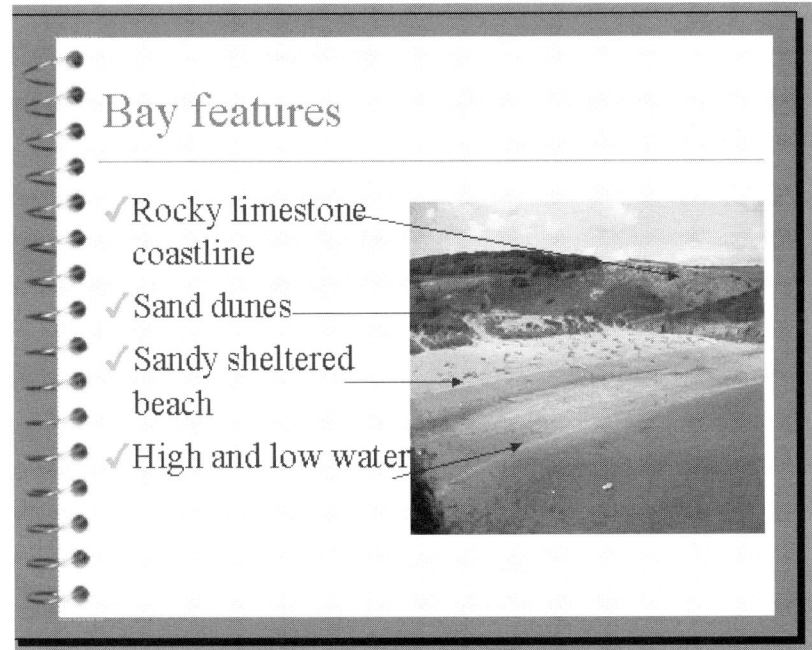

A presentation slide in MS Office Powerpoint using text, an imported photo and drawing tools.

a set sequence once it is started. The left mouse button moves the sequence on by one slide. The right mouse button moves it back by one slide.

■ Clip art or other illustrations can be imported either from the program's own bank of resources or from other programs.

■ The presentation can be run either at

fixed time intervals or controlled manually using the mouse.

■ Slides can be made to appear in a variety of ways and at different speeds, for example, as an image that slides from the left, appears as blinds or dissolves. Key points of text appear either at once or are activated by the speaker. Previous text can be dimmed out as new text appears.

■ An LCD or projector is used to give the presentation on a wall screen.

■ The presentation can be saved on a floppy disc then run on a computer with the basic facility to show the presentation. This can be as a viewer only, without the facility to create or edit the program.

■ Handouts can be made of the presentation. This can be done as text, or as thumbnail copies of the slides.

2.4.2 Presentation in the classroom

Although the result can be impressive, the skills needed to create a presentation are minimal. The main need is to ensure that the text and illustrations are appropriate for this kind of presentation. This involves using a bullet point style of writing, preferably using a font size that is large enough to be read easily. A size of at least 32 should be used in a classroom. Using this bullet point style of writing may even help to present the key points more clearly.

There is some risk that the quality of the presentation can mask the quality of the content. This however, is mainly a problem when using this kind of presentation with an audience who are not familiar with it.

The main problems in a classroom are in setting up the equipment and using an LCD panel or projector, including ensuring that there is a good blackout. A permanent setup is perhaps the most efficient way to use this kind of program, though a portable computer projector and laptop computer can be a relatively easy way to overcome these problems.

Word processor to presentation

A document written in Word can be changed to a Powerpoint presentation by using the *Present it* icon. This is found by opening the *Microsoft toolbar* in *View*. The conversion is best when the document has been typed in short phrases. There is also the facility to convert text from Powerpoint to Word.

Key words

- multi-media authoring; using still and moving images and sound to present material
- button; a shape on the screen that gives a command to go to another screen or to perform an action
- hotspot; a place on the screen that causes an action
- hotword or hypertext; a word that when clicked, causes an action, e.g. to launch another file or go to another card
- card or slide; one page of a file
- stack; the cards that make a file in the Hyperstudio Multi-media authoring program

2.5 Multi-media authoring

Multi-media authoring is a way of presenting information in a way that;
- uses text, illustrations, sound and video
- is interactive for the user
- can access information in a different order

Some multi-media authoring programs are simple to operate and are well within the capabilities of relatively young pupils and their teachers. They are also priced within a school budget.

2.5.1 Basic skills

The basic skills needed to use a multi-media authoring program are little more than;
- knowledge of word processing
- familarity with the software
- a knowledge of file management to import art work
- the creative ability to make effective use of multi-media facilities
- a logical approach to structuring material.

Most of these skills will have been developed when using other basic ICT applications.

Multi media authoring in Illuminatus

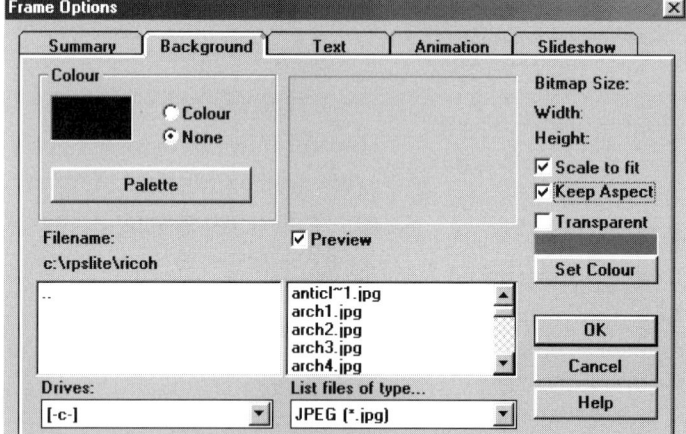

2.5.2 Making multi-media

A multi-media presentation is made by using the different functions contained in the program. These are items such as buttons, frames, text and drawing tools.

- Slides are built up as a set of cards to make a stack.
- Alternative routes through the stack can be chosen by creating buttons that activate choices.

- Different types of media such as sound, video, text and photos can be included.
- Simple animations can be created or imported.

- Links can be made to resources on the Internet or to launch other files.
- The finished product can be shown as a form of presentation.

2.6 Special purpose programs

A number of special purpose programs are available. These involve activities such as;

- writing reports
- writing worksheets.

They have the advantage of containing banks of comments or templates. Even these can be customised to meet individual needs and to remove their standardized appearance.

2.7 Video-conferencing

Video-conferencing is a method of visual and audio communication by computer. This can be a useful way to bring people in contact with others without travelling.

- A digital video camera takes images of a speaker at one computer. The images are then transmitted to one or more computers in other places.
- People at both computers can talk to each other, though there is a short time lag in sound.
- Information can be presented on screen at the same time as the speaker. This is done by using a notebook that can contain text, photos and other images. The speaker can highlight parts of the screen at the same time as speaking.

2.8 Pupil activities

The range of applications associated with text can be used by pupils for;

- creating, sending or presenting documents
- storing information
- giving presentations
- word play activities

2.8.1 Creating, sending or presenting documents

Every part of the process involved in writing a document can be done on screen.

- Ideas can initially be brainstormed then rearranged. Irrelevant ideas can be removed and new ones added.
- Summary notes can be written, either from a book or from another program.

- Rough drafts can be made to clarify the main ideas. There is no need to work in any particular order as work can be saved then restructured later.
- A final document can be produced to a professional standard. This can be a newspaper page activity, an extended enquiry or any other type of written activity.
- Finished documents can be printed, read directly from the screen or sent as Email.

Key words

◆ Alt and Tab; the Alt key and the Tab key (above Caps lock) on the keyboard

◆ clipboard; a part of the computer's memory that holds information (see notebook)

Create a text box in Word

◆ A box can be put into position when working in Word by clicking on the program's *Drawing tools* option in the toolbar.

◆ The *text box* option is then selected.

◆ A box is drawn on the page where text is to be entered.

◆ The box can be made invisible by putting a clear outline around the text box using the *line colour* option.

◆ To put text into the box, click anywhere inside the box then type.

◆ The box can be edited to a different size and shape by clicking on the box, then on the border around it, then dragging the handles.

◆ The box can be moved to a new position by clicking on the border line then dragging it across the page.

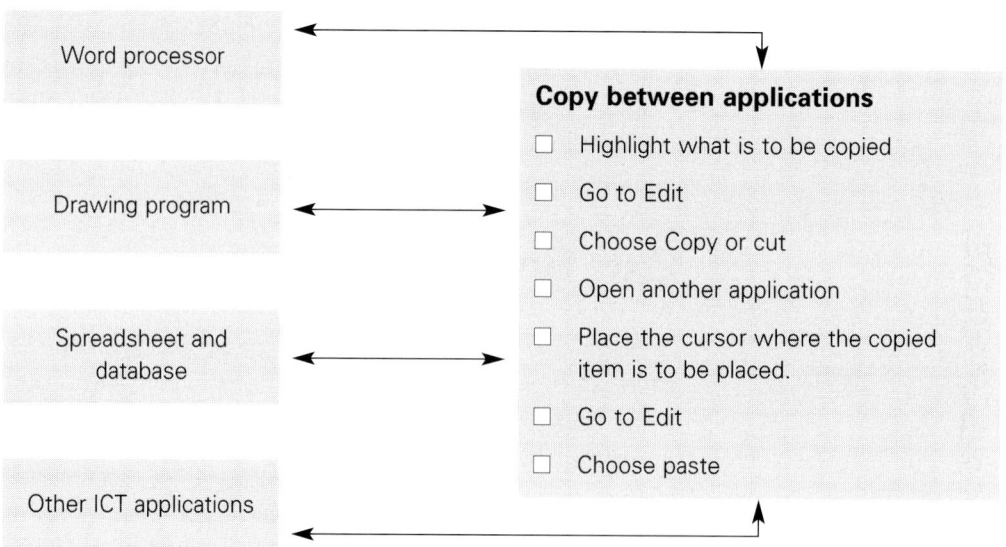

Word processor

Drawing program

Spreadsheet and database

Other ICT applications

Copy between applications

☐ Highlight what is to be copied

☐ Go to Edit

☐ Choose Copy or cut

☐ Open another application

☐ Place the cursor where the copied item is to be placed.

☐ Go to Edit

☐ Choose paste

Copy or Cut and Paste between most applications

2.8.2 Storing information

The ability to copy and store selected information is useful when working with other programs such as CDs. Information can be quickly scanned by eye then copied so that it can be read in more detail later. This includes copying information from the Internet.

● Some programs have their own copy facility that copies text or illustrations into a clipboard. This allows them to be pasted into a word processor. Either complete or selected sections of text can be copied and pasted in this way. The same can be done with other programs using standard Edit and cut or copy functions.

● Information can then be adapted with selected items copied as direct quotations. Pupils however, must be strongly advised to give the original source of all items that are copied.

2.8.3 Giving presentations

Group work can be an effective way to generate ideas and to solve problems. A presentation program can be used to help the group to report back to other groups.

● A program such as Powerpoint can be used to present key ideas and illustrations.

● A word processor using a large font can also be used for presentations. Key points written as text can be scrolled down using the scroll bar.

● A presentation can be created using a multi-media authoring program. Different members of a group can take responsibility for different aspects of the work such as taking photos with a digital camera, recording sound, creating animations and filming with a video camera.

2.8.4 Word play activities

Worksheets can be created on a word processor then saved on a network as *Read Only* files. This gives opportunities for a range of simple word play activities.

● Sentences with missing words can be written either as normal text or with hidden text boxes. The words can be either left to the pupils to write, or they can be written by the teacher. Words can be highlighted by the pupil then dragged to the correct place.

● 'Heads' and 'tails' activities can be written using the facility to move individual words, phrases or whole sentences to different places on the screen.

● Spelling can be tested by allowing pupils to use a spell check. Words such as 'vegetation' and 'Mediterranean' can be written correctly or incorrectly for the pupil to check. Many place names or technical terms are not included though these can be added to the word bank.

Many similar types of activities could be developed and saved on a network's hard drive.

2.9 Conclusions

There are many opportunities to make use of generic word processing and different types of presentation program. For the teacher, documents can be written and saved then easily adapted. Printing the document is one option, but pupils can also be asked to work with the document on screen at the same time as working with a different program. For the pupils, they give opportunities to make changes to their ideas and to enhance the quality of their final documents. Because so much of the presentation graphics is already provided, time can be devoted instead to the content of the work.

Pupil activity; settlement geography

1   Use one or more CD encyclopaedias such as Encarta to find out about the population and present functions of London and New York.

    a)   Briefly read then select and copy text about both cities into a word processor.

    b)   Photos and other illustrations such as maps can also be copied.

    c)   For any item you have copied, make sure to say where it came from.

2   Carefully read all the information you have copied.

    a)   Delete all information that is not relevant to the task.

    b)   Write your own report about the population and functions of both cities. Describe how they are similar in some ways, but different in others.
Do this by creating a document in a word processor.
Population and other statistics could be entered in a table in the document.
Special quotations could be included from the research sources if they are relevant.
Maps or other illustrations could also be imported into the wordprocessed document

Pupil activity; volcanic landscapes

1 The first part of this activity is to check that words to do with volcanic landscapes are spelt correctly

  a) Run a spell check on these sets of words.
    Delete the words that are spelt wrongly.

lavar	lava	larva
erruption	erupsion	eruption
granit	granite	granete
volcano	volcanoe	vulcano

2 This activity should be carried out on the computer.
  Move the missing words to the right place by highlighting them, then dragging them into the correct position. They will drop into hidden text boxes when the left mouse button is released.

A cone-shaped mountain made of lava and other volcanic rocks is called a _____ .

The mountain is made higher every time there is an _____ .

This sends streams of _____ *rock flowing down the slopes.*

The flowing rock usually cools quite quickly so there is no time for _____ *to grow.*

A typical rock formed in this way is called _____ .

A volcanic rock that cools more slowly deep underground is called _____ .

Missing words
eruption   crystals   granite   volcano   molten   basalt

Note
The spaces have been made by creating text boxes with clear outlines.
To enter a missing word, simply highlight, drag then drop it in the right space.

3 Using data

3.1 Data in geography

Raw data in the form of statistics from both primary and secondary sources help geographers understand processes, describe patterns and test hypotheses. This raw data can be put into a computer program that facilitates its presentation and analysis. The two types of applications used for this work are spreadsheets and databases.

3.1.1 Features of ICT

Several features of ICT can be useful when handling data, especially when the amounts are large.
- speed and automatic functions; to set up templates to measure, record and to carry out calculations quickly
- capacity and range; to handle large amounts of data and to present it
- provisionality; to make changes to data, including obtaining a rapid response to those changes
- interactivity; the ability to get a quick result with dynamic feedback.

3.1.2 Processes in handling data

This chapter looks at the following processes in relation to handling data;
- data logging
- data recording
- data presentation
- data processing

3. 2 Data logging

Raw data can be collected using ICT in four main ways.
- A data logger uses peripheral hardware such as sensors or counters to take an electronic record of the data. This can be done either directly into a computer or collected remotely 'in the field' then downloaded later.
- A Global Positioning System (GPS) hand held monitor can be used to log field data. This can record both position and variables. Although relatively expensive at the moment, this kind of technology should become more easily available and affordable.
- A weather station uses sensors and other instruments to measure and log weather variables. Figures for temperature, pressure and wind speed is then fed directly into a computer.
- Data can be recorded in the field onto a palmtop computer.

3.3 Data recording

Raw data can be recorded into two main types of program;

■ spreadsheets
■ databases.

Although spreadsheets and databases have some features in common, there are also some key differences. Both can be used to record and store raw data. This is done in cells in a way that looks similar on the screen. Both have some functions to present and process data.

A spreadsheet however, is mainly intended to be a table on which all the data is written and stored. This is different from a database which stores data in the form of separate records, like on separate cards. A record for example, can contain different items of data about a country. The records and individual items of data can then be brought together in different combinations.

Some data handling programs are generic programs such as the Excel spreadsheet and the Access database in MSOffice, or similar programs in the MSWorks suite of programs. Others are written for a single purpose, often as part of a larger and specialised program such as for recording and processing field study data.

3.3.1 Data on a spreadsheet

A spreadsheet is an electronic table on which data is entered. Calculations can then be made and graphs drawn.

- Spreadsheets store data in any combination of three forms, text, numbers and formulae.
- The data is entered on a table that is divided into rows (across the table) and columns (down the table). The width of columns and the depth of rows can be changed to suit the space needed by the data.
- Data is put into boxes called cells. The reference for each cell is given by its column (A, B, C, etc.) then its row (1, 2, 3 etc.), for example, cell B4.
- The size of the table in generic programs extends well beyond what is seen on the screen at any one time. The total table is seen by using the scroll bar.
- The amount of data that can be stored is vast. In MS Excel, there are 256 columns and 16384 rows, giving 4194304 cells in which to enter data. This is usually sufficient for most geography work in school!
- The size of a cell can be changed to suit the data.
- The data in rows and columns can be cut or copied and pasted into new rows or columns to bring different sets of data together.

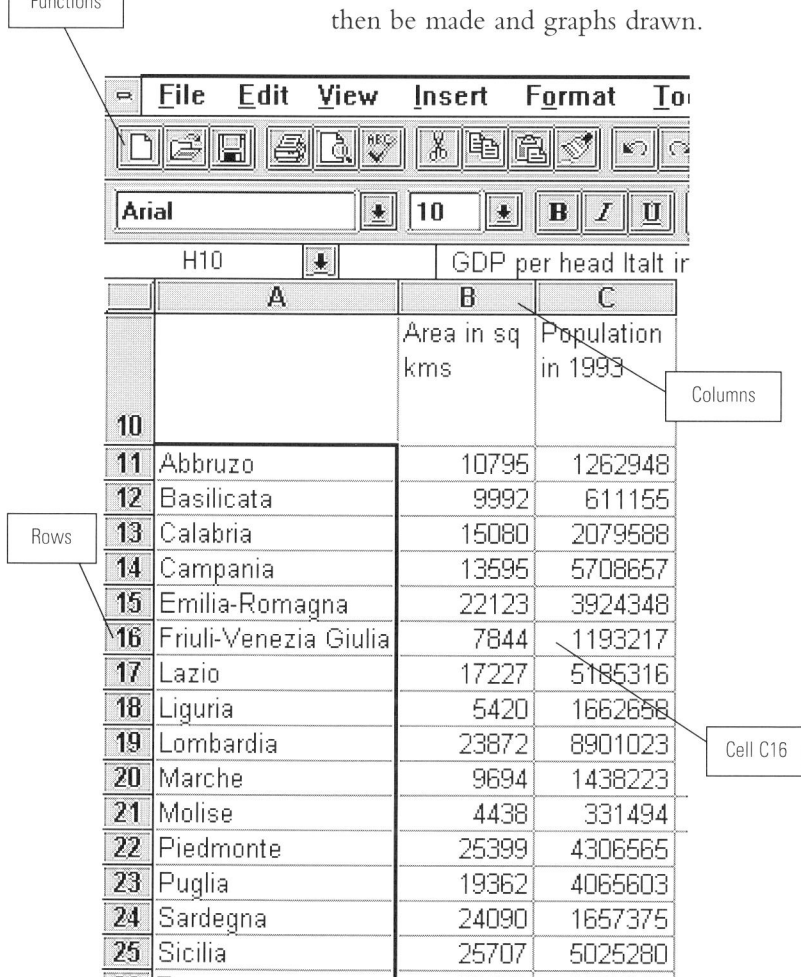

The Excel spreadsheet in the MS Office suite of programs

Spreadsheets

♦ book; one or more sheets of data in a spreadsheet to make a complete datafile

♦ cell; a space for recording an individual item of data

♦ column; a vertical line of cells

♦ row; a line of cells across the table

♦ sheet; one page of data

♦ table; a grid on which data is centered

Text in a spreadsheet or database

Text can be written into cells in the same way as figures. This may be useful if data is in both numeric and alpha-numeric form. It can also be an alternative to using a table in a word processor. A problem however, is that moving text between cells involves copying or cutting and pasting instead of simply highlighting and dragging.

● In some programs, one or more sheets make up a book of data.

● The order of the data can be rearranged, for example by putting it in alphabetical or numerical order. A spreadsheet however, does not have all the capabilities of a database to bring different pieces of raw data together in a variety of ways.

● A simple search function can be used to locate an item of data. This is done by choosing the *Edit* and *Find* option.

● The most difficult part of handling raw data is in making decisions about the exact nature and form in which the data is to be collected. This is what determines the headings and appearance of the spreadsheet.

● The most time-consuming part is typing in the data. This is also the part where most errors are likely to occur. Once an error is embedded, it will obviously affect all calculations that are carried out using formulae.

3.3.2 Databases

Although the cells and general appearance of a database have some similarities to a spreadsheet when entering data, it is set up in a different way.

● Each set of data is called a record. For example, a record can be for a country, for a river or any other feature.

● A field describes the heading for each piece of data in the record. These are entered on the vertical stack of cells. A field could be for population, birth rates and GNP for a country.

● The names of records and fields need to be set up before the data is collected. The database is then set up under these headings.

● Some generic databases have templates designed for different purposes. Some may be suitable for geographical data, or they can be adapted to make them suitable. Wizards or assistants may help you create your database.

CSV files

A CSV (comma separated value) file is a file format that can be used to save raw data.

Data saved in this format can be accessed by different spreadsheet programs, no matter what type of program has been used to create the file.

A CSV file is converted to make it accessible to a different program by following some basic screen commands. Lines for example, can be inserted where there are commas to show where the different columns are to be inserted.

Raw data on river discharge and rainfall for example, is produced in CSV format by the Environment Agency and can be made available to teachers.

Entering data on a spreadsheet

♦ To enter raw data, first click on the cell. Then type in the data. The action is confirmed by pressing the *Enter* key, or by clicking on a new cell to enter more data.

♦ The alignment of data in the cell can be changed, e.g. to move it to the top or bottom, or horizontal or vertical. To do this, click back on the cell then either click on *Format* then cells, or use the right mouse button to access the format cell option. In the *Format Cells* window, choose *Alignment* then click on the options you want.

♦ To change the width of a column or the depth of a row, position the cursor exactly on the dividing line between the cell numbers or letters e.g. between B or 2. When the cursor changes to a cross, drag the dividing line to a new width or depth.

♦ Text can be made to fit a cell without changing the column width. Do this in *Cell Format* and choose the *Wrap Text* option. This increases the cell depth to make the data fit.

● The purpose of a database is to bring different pieces of data together in a variety of combinations. This is done by using a query to select the data needed. The query can choose the type and range of data that is required. The program then sorts through the records to find and present only that data.

● Different datafiles can be linked to form a powerful relational database. This can access and link data at different levels within the databases.

3.3.3 Special databases

Some databases are pre-designed to be part of particular programs.

● Census data for example, is available as database files. Data can be queried, sorted, and sometimes also graphed and mapped. From some programs, the data can be copied and pasted into a generic spreadsheet or database.

● Some special purpose fieldwork programs contain databases and spreadsheets on which to enter raw data. This can then be processed using formulae that are specific to the fieldwork, for example to work out a river's hydraulic radius or discharge.

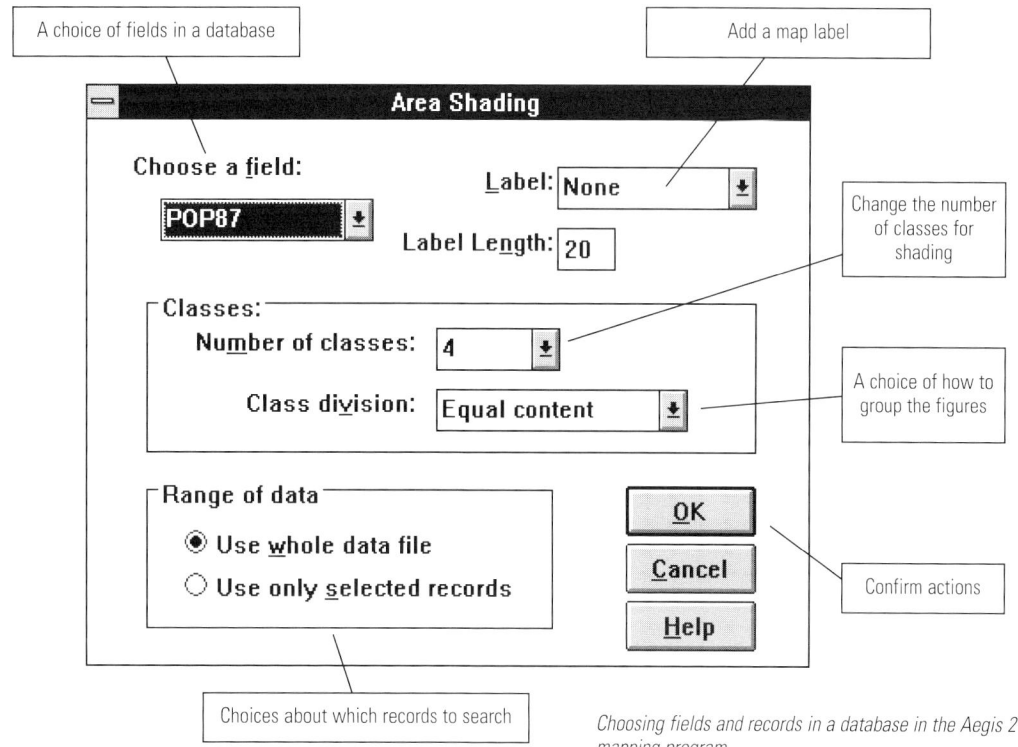

Choosing fields and records in a database in the Aegis 2 mapping program

3.4 Presenting data

Spreadsheets and databases present data in the form of tables, without the need to do anything more to the data. They also offer an extensive choice of different types of graphs. These can be useful to identify trends and patterns. Further statistical analysis can then be carried out using formulae.

■ A simple way to make raw data visually more effective on the original table is to use the colour palette. Numbers, text, cells or blocks of cells in rows or columns can be colour-coded to make them easier to identify on a screen.

■ Data can be graphed in many different styles. The main problem is in choosing the most appropriate style of graph for your purpose. A choice is offered with one style given as a default. This is the one that the program selects as being suitable, but your choice may be different.

Drawing a graph in the Excel spreadsheet

- ◆ Click and drag over all the data to be graphed.

- ◆ Click on the graph tool (the chart wizard) in the toolbar.

- ◆ Move the pointer to any empty space on the spreadsheet and drag out a rectangle, then release the mouse button.

- ◆ Make a choice about the type of graph from the selection offered in the options window.

- ◆ Make choices about the ways the data is to appear and give the graph a label.

- ◆ The graph is then drawn automatically in the space outlined.

- ◆ The graph is in an editable box. This means it can be cut and pasted to another application. This is done by choosing Edit then copy, followed by Edit and paste in the other application.

- ◆ Details of the graph such as its labels can also be changed by double clicking on the handles around the box. Its size and shape can be changed by clicking on the handles around the box.

Birth and death rates in Italy

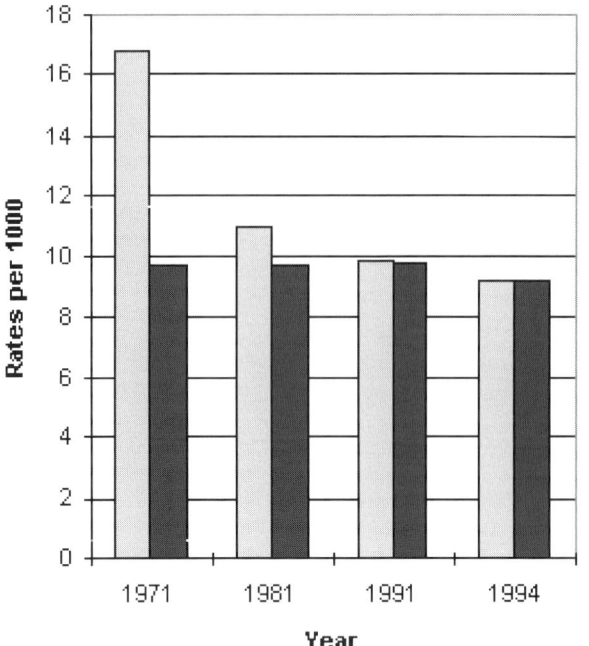

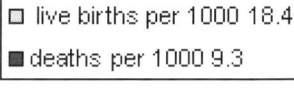
Bar graph of birth and death rates in Italy

year	live births per 1000	deaths per 1000
1961	18.4	9.3
1971	16.8	9.7
1981	11	9.7
1991	9.9	9.8
1994	9.2	9.2

The area in '000 hectares for Italy's main physical features

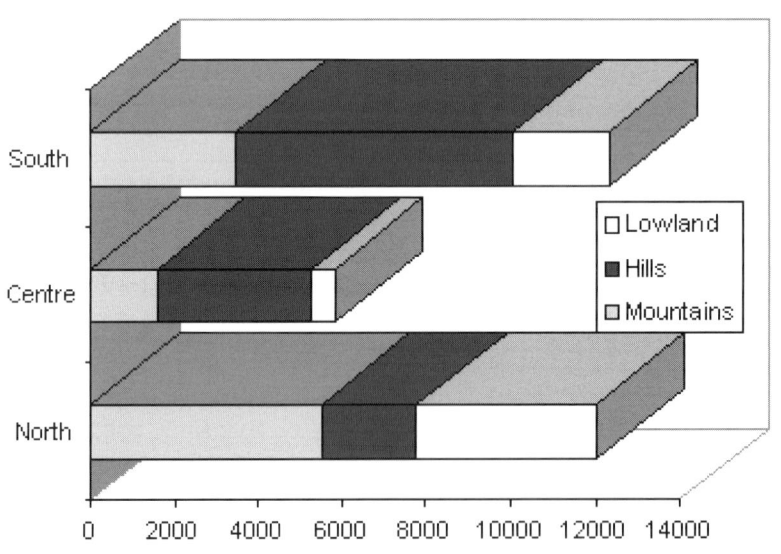

A 3-D divided bar graph of land use in Italy

- ■ On a spreadsheet, a graph to show two sets of data is easily drawn when the data is adjacent. If the data is in columns or rows that are not adjacent, they can both be highlighted by holding down the *Control (CTRL)* key. An alternative is to copy then paste the two rows or columns so that they are beside each other.

- ■ Any graph can be copied and pasted into a word processor, drawing program or other generic program. A larger document combining commentary text and graphics can then be created.

Creating rows and columns in an Excel spreadsheet

- ◆ A new row or column can be added later for either new data or to cut and paste data so that it appears together.

- ◆ First click on the letter or number along the row or column identification line.

- ◆ Then click on the Insert option. This gives the choice of a new row or column.

3.5 Processing data

Once statistical data has been entered on a spreadsheet or database, it can be processed by using formulae. These can be used to give totals, percentages or for any kind of calculation. Words, called alpha-numeric data, can be processed to a limited extent by sorting into alphabetical order.

Writing formulae

◆ Click in a cell where you want the figure to appear.

◆ Always begin by entering the equals sign (=).

◆ Write the formula by giving the cell references (B4 etc.) then the way the formula is to be worked out.

◆ Add is +, take away is -, times is * and divide is /.

◆ The same formula can be applied to other rows or columns of data by highlighting the cell where the formula has been written, then dragging a handle across to other empty cells, or by copying and pasting the cell.

3.5.1 Using formulae

Formulae can be worked out either by clicking on an icon, for example on the Autosum icon in Excel to give a total, or by entering a formula in the cell.

● Totals for a row or column of data can be obtained by highlighting the figures required and typing a formula in a vacant cell. Another way to do this is to use the Autosum on the toolbar.

● By changing one item of data, a new total or other calculation will be automatically worked out. This is because the formula works by identifying cell numbers, no matter what data is contained in them.

● Different types of average can be worked out, for example finding the mean figure for temperature data. To do this in Excel, click on an empty cell, then write
=AVERAGE (first cell :last cell)
or use the function wizard to obtain the mean. Most programs have a similar list of formulae from which to choose, e.g. the Claris Works spreadsheet on Apple computers or Results on Acorns.

● Relationships between data can be obtained using correlation formulae. To do this either highlight the two sets of data using the Control key or copy and paste the data sets so that they are beside each other.

● By making a change to one of the variables, the effect can be to ask questions about how different items of data relate to each other. This is a form of modelling, for example, to show how a change in river velocity would affect discharge.

● Formulae can be dependent on other formulae. The effect of this is to provide results of relationships between data that would otherwise be complex to calculate.

Functions in the Excel spreadsheet

| Autosum for totals | Function wizard for formulae | Sort text or figures in order, A-Z or lowest to highest | Sort text or figures in order, Z-A or from highest to lowest | Graph wizard |

3.6 Spreadsheets and databases in geography

There are several reasons for using a spreadsheet or database by pupils in geography. They must first however, understand which one is likely to be the most suitable for their needs.

- Spreadsheets and databases give a clear, ordered and flexible way in which to record data. This can be useful when handling large amounts of field study or secondary data.
- The data can be stored on a floppy disc or hard drive for future use. Access is quick and editing can be carried out neatly with automatic changes made to calculations that have already been set up. Making changes to variables can help to model effects of change.
- The data can be moved into another program such as a word processor, or even between different spreadsheets and databases.
- Data can be exchanged by E-mail with pupils in other schools, for example, sending data about local environmental conditions, traffic or river flows.
- There is a range of functions that are quick to use such as drawing graphs and processing the data. This should provide more time to analyse and evaluate the data.
- The finished product, whether as a table or as a graph, has a professional appearance that is the same for all pupils. This can be important in geography because of its emphasis on visually presented data.

3.7 Issues in using spreadsheets and databases

As with mapping and drawing programs, spreadsheets and databases both offer new opportunities and create new issues to be resolved.

3.7.1 New opportunities

Pupils have access to styles of graphs that are difficult to draw by hand. They may however, be presented with choices that they do not fully understand. This can happen when selecting a type of graph from a generic spreadsheet. The same is true of statistical formulae. This may call for a different emphasis on the kind of skills that need to be taught.

3.7.2 Assessment issues

As with other uses of ICT, there are several issues with regard to assessment.

- Work produced by different pupils using spreadsheets and databases can be identical. This need not be a problem when the work has been done by a group. It may however, be hard to know who has done the recording, presenting and statistical calculations. These are all very different processes that may need to be separately assessed.

- The written analysis and evaluation at least ought to be recognisable as being individual, though even this may be typed in a word processor.

- The criteria for assessment need to be considered carefully as they may be different from the criteria that would be appropriate to using hand drawn methods.

- Problems of access to computers between different pupils may as usual, be a further complication.

3.8 Conclusions

The use of both generic and topic-specific spreadsheets and databases gives pupils studying geography, access to a range of techniques to record, present and process data that are difficult to do by more traditional methods. New skills need to be taught so that pupils can make proper use of these techniques. There also needs to be new thinking over how work done in this way can be assessed.

Sample activity; population change

1 This activity is about how the population is changing in a selection of countries.

a) Open the spreadsheet and study the data. Work out a suitable structure for data, for example, where to list the countries and where to list the figures. Type the data into the cells.

b) Use the sort function to arrange the countries in order to show the countries with the highest estimated population totals for the year 1995 at the top.
Copy the columns showing this data.
Open a word processor document and paste the data into it.

c) Go back to your spreadsheet.
Draw a graph to show the birth and death rates for the countries on the spreadsheet. Make sure to choose a style of graph that shows the data in a way that is plain and clear.
To show the names of the countries in the graph, you may need to insert a new column by using the Control key or by copying then pasting the names of the countries so they are beside the birth and death rate columns.

d) Draw a second graph of the same data. This time, choose a style of graph that looks more interesting. It may be a style that makes the figures more difficult to read and compare.

c) Choose the graph you think is the most helpful for showing the data.
Copy then paste it into your wordprocessed document.
What does the graph tell you about the birth and death rates in different countries?

2 Process the figures by working out some calculations.

a) Work out the mean birth rates and death rates for the countries.

b) Choose and apply different background colours to the cells to show which figures are above and also below the averages (means).

3 Imagine you were to set up a database for the figures on the spreadsheet.
What title would you give to each record? What headings would you use to describe the fields?

Population data for ten countries

Country name	Total population for 1980	Total population for 1995	Birth rate	Death rate	Average annual % change
Australia	18.1	14.7	14	8	1.4
Brazil	161.4	121.3	26	8	1.4
Egypt	64.1	40.1	31	9	4.0
France	58.3	53.8	13	10	0.8
Japan	125.2	116.8	12	8	0.3
Kenya	28.4	16.6	47	10	3.3
Zambia	9.5	5.8	50	12	3.3
Pakistan	143.6	85.3	42	11	5.1
United Kingdom	58.3	56.3	14	12	0.4

Sample Activity; industrial location

1 A company wants to build a new factory at a new location.
Four possible locations have been investigated (A, B, C and D).
Costs to run the factory during a year have been worked out. These are shown on the grid below. Figures are in £m.

	Transporting raw materials (by rail)	Delivering products to customers (by road)	Cost of renting land	Workers' wages
Site A	3.3	5.1	0.5	1.1
Site B	1.3	3.3	0.3	0.9
Site C	4.2	2.8	1.1	1.2
Site D	2.1	3.4	0.6	0.8

a) Enter the figures for the different sites on a spreadsheet.

b) Work out the total cost of running the factory at each site for a year. The description below refers to Excel. Other programs have different ways of working.

   To do this, first insert another column for the total costs for each site.
   Then enter a formula to add up the different costs for each site.
   Do this with = cell+cell+ cell, for example, B3 + C4 etc.
   Another way to get the total is to highlight the data then use the Autosum.
   Drag the formula down to apply it to the other three sites.

c) Which site would have the lowest running costs? You could highlight the site by applying a different colour to the cell where the site is listed.

2 The company thinks that in a few year's time, there will be tolls to pay on all motorways, and that the cost of fuel will go up. This will make transporting the products twice as expensive from all the sites.

a) Work out what the total costs would be if the transport costs of the products doubled.
   To do this, you need to insert an extra column beside the total you have already worked out.
   Then enter the appropriate formula, e.g. in Excel = cell+(cell⋆2)+cell.
   Drag the formula down to apply to the other three sites.

b) Look at the new totals to see which site would now be the cheapest to run?
   You could insert a new column beside the list of sites, enter the totals in the new cells, then sort the list using the sort function in the Data option. Make sure to highlight the columns with both the site letter and the totals, and arrange the list by order of the figures.

3 Think about using this data to make your decision.

a) Explain why these costs might be the most important ones?

b) Can you think of any other reasons or costs that might be important?

c) What other changes to the costs might there be in future years? Why might some changes affect some sites more than others?

4 Think of another change that might affect the costs of either all the sites, or might only happen at one.

a) Make a prediction too about which site will now be the cheapest.

b) Change one or more figures in the table to show the change.

c) What effect has this had on the result? Was your prediction right or wrong?

4 Photographs on screen

4.1 Photos for geography

*P*hotos are an invaluable resource in geography, whether to add colour and other detail to a place that can not be visited, or as a record of field study work. All types of photos, whether ground, oblique or vertical air views, can be put onto a computer screen. There are many ways to do this from different types of originals. All that needs to be done is to ensure that they are in digital form. With appropriate peripherals such as a digital camera or scanner, this is a relatively simple operation.

Digital photos

- ◆ A photo in digital form can be read by a computer in the same way that text and any other digital image can be read.

- ◆ Photos can be captured directly by a digital camera or copied onto a scanner.

- ◆ Photos on a CD are already in digital form.

4.2 Using digital photos

Some reasons why working with photos on screen can be an advantage relate to;
- numbers and choice
- creating photo trails
- independent use by pupils
- changing photo size
- changing a photo's content
- costs

4.2.1 Numbers and choice

Using photos on a computer screen gives access to a number and choice that has previously not been practical.
- Some photobase CDs contain in the order of 2000 photos. Photos are also included in most general and subject-specific software.
- Search procedures can be made easy with a search function or a 'hot word' index that takes the user immediately to the image they want. Doing this can be more immediate and more convenient than research in books.
- Programs with a preview function allows an image to be loaded quickly, instead of waiting for the full image to be loaded.
- Greater choice should mean that the most appropriate image is used, as well as giving the user a greater level of input to the work. A risk is that the choice becomes overwhelming.

4.2.2 Photo trails

A photo trail is a pre-selected set of photos chosen from a larger collection. Some subject-specific programs have photo trails as a built-in function. There is also a photo trail function on some generic programs such as on photo processing programs.
- The process of selecting photos from an extensive photo bank can be stimulating and enjoyable but also time consuming and diverting. A pre-selected trail can overcome this problem.
- Pupils are likely to make constructive use of only a limited number of photos on any one topic.
- Photo trails can be stored for repeated use.
- Photo trails can be differentiated as required.
- Trails can also be created by a pupil as part of a presentation.

4.2.3 Independent use

Working with a computer gives the pupil a greater degree of independence in their learning.

- Access to an extensive range of photos means that pupils can make their own choices over places and topics to study. Learning templates with general guidance provided by the teacher are needed for this to be done effectively.
- Pupils can work at a pace that is appropriate to their abilities. This is in contrast to the pace that is needed when slides are shown by a teacher.
- Photos can be immediately recalled if further work needs to be done.
- On some programs, an audio commentary is provided to complement accompanying text or captions. This is especially useful to help weak readers.

4.2.4 Photo size

The size of photos on screen can be changed easily, depending on the software being used to process it.

- Unlike a photocopier, there is no additional cost to enlarging or reducing image size.
- The large size of a photo on screen allows for greater visual appeal and impact.
- There is often an option to see photos either as part screen or in full screen view.
- Programs that process photos can magnify sections of a photo using a zoom facility. The photo can then be explored by moving to different parts with a scroll bar or grabber tool. Too much magnification however, loses quality, though the extent of loss partly depends on the density at which the photo has been captured and saved.

A photo taken with a digital camera

An enlarged part of the photo showing how the image breaks down into individual pixels when magnified

4.2.5 Changing a photo

A photo can be changed once it is put into a drawing or photo processing program. This is best done in a program that was designed to process photos. It can also be done in basic drawing programs such as Paint or Paintbrush in PCs or Draw in Acorn.

- Features can be added, recoloured, enhanced, replaced or removed.
- Additional lines, text and other drawings can be superimposed on a photo.
- Any amount or type of changes can be made without destroying the original image.

Changes to a coastal landform made by copying sections of the images then pasting them into new positions, then using the painting tools to blend in the new sections. This was done using the basic Paintbrush program in Windows 3,1

4.2.6 Costs

Photos on disc have several cost advantages over hard copy photos, though it is not easy to compare the two.

- Digital photos do not have the same problems of storage and handling so they can not be destroyed, other than on a corrupted disc or by losing the disc.
- Many more photos can be bought on one CD than would be available in a book at a comparable price.

- Multiple copies of colour photos can be hard to produce. Copies are not needed when using a program on a computer network.
- The main cost can be one of paying for enough hard drive or other disc space on which to store photos. Refer to section **4.3.4** for further details of saving photos.
- Other costs involve the hardware and software needed to capture, store and view the photos.

Refer to section **4.3.4** for further details of saving photos.

Key words

- ◆ scanner; a peripheral to copy pictures and change them into digital form

- ◆ digital camera; a camera to take pictures in digital form

- ◆ acquire; to take an image from a scanner or digital camera and bring it into the photo processing software.

- ◆ capture; to take an image, or part of an image, from the screen

- ◆ resolution; the density of the image, taking more disc space to save better quality images

- ◆ format; a way that a file is saved, e.g. as a BMP (bitmap) or a more compressed file such as a Tif or JPEG.

4.3 Sources of digital photos

There are many different sources of photos. These include;

- from photobase CDs and other programs
- scanning and slide copying
- digital camera

4.3.1 From programs

Photos can be taken from different kinds of programs in different ways.

- Photos are included in most CDs and other programs. Many of these have copy and paste functions to move selected items to other programs. There may also be a print function to obtain a hard copy.
- Photos can be copied and saved from the Internet.
- A 'snapshot' of the whole screen can be taken using the *Print Screen* key in PCs, or *Snapshot* command in Apple. The image can then be pasted into a drawing program. The whole photo, or a part that is needed, can then be cut out and saved or imported directly into another document.

4.3.2 Scanning and slide copying

Photos can be converted to digital form by different methods of scanning. The processes of doing this are all handled easily by the software and hardware. Knowledge of the terms involved in capturing and acquiring the images is useful.

- A scanner can copy photo prints, maps or any other kind of image.
- A slide copier can change 35 mm slides or print negatives into digital form.

Using the Print Screen key

- ◆ Find and show the photo on the screen
- ◆ Click on the *Print Scrn* key (also written as *Print Screen*)
- ◆ Open a drawing program such as Paint, Paintbrush, Paintshop Pro or another drawing program
- ◆ Copy the whole screen using the paste function in *Edit*
- ◆ Cut out the photo or part of the photo you want, then copy and paste it into a new file. An alternative is to use a rubber from the toolbox to remove what you do not want from the screen.

- The quality of the image mainly depends on the resolution being used to capture it. The highest quality photos can take up a large amount of disc space.
- The cost of a scanner is now so low as to be affordable by almost any budget, though quality of image may be an issue.

4.3.3 Digital camera

A digital camera captures images directly in a form that can then be put on a computer screen.

- The process is quick and immediate in contrast to waiting for prints to be developed.
- A poor image can be immediately erased and another photo taken to replace it.

Understanding file formats

- The user need not know details of how different file formats work or even what they mean.

- It is important to know that some save files in a compressed form, taking less storage space than others.

- Some programs do not accept all file formats. The formats that are acceptable can be seen when saving files by looking in the command to *save file as type*.

- A zip facility is a way of saving files in a compressed form.

- BMP (bitmaps) are one common file format, though these take up a large amout of storage space.

- JPEG (Joint Photographic Experts Group) images are a compressed way to save an image, though not all programs are able to handle them. There are also many other file formats that can compress them, taking less disc space to save an image.

- format; a way that a file is saved, e.g. as a BMP (bitmap) or a more compressed file such as a Tif or JPEG.

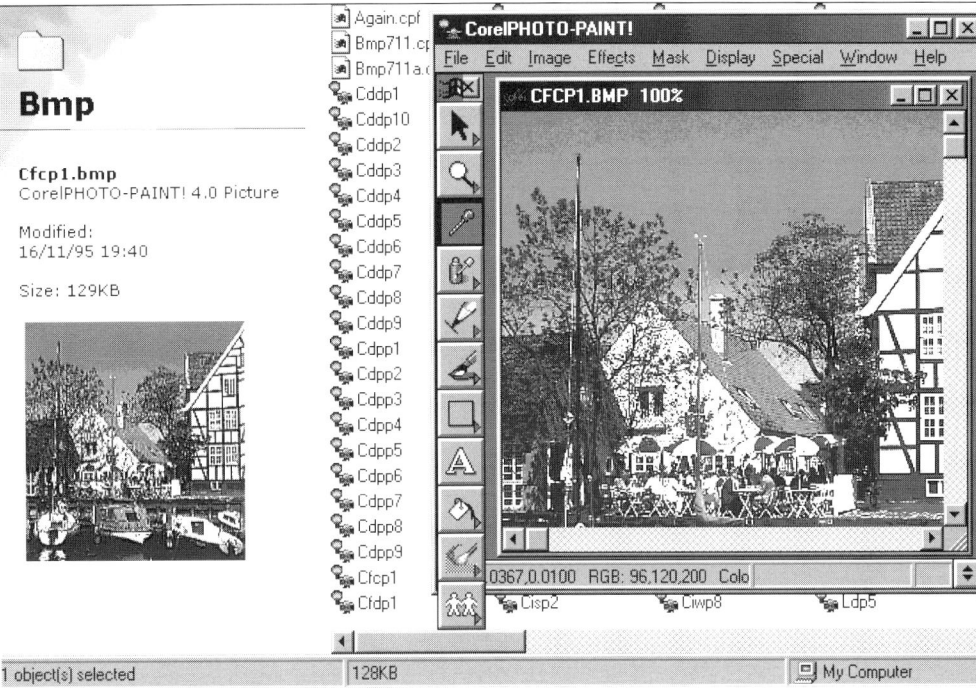

Finding photos from CDs in File Manager (Windows 3.1)

A digital camera

- A hand held camera that takes photos in a digital form

- As easy to operate as a normal basic camera

- Photos are stored on a small disc , a normal floppy disc or on a memory chip in the camera. The number of images that can be taken before downloading depends on the quality of the image taken. Reasonable results can usually give about 50 images. For much higher quality, the number may only be 15.

- Photos are transferred to the computer's hard drive and stored

- Photos can be changed to enhance light, colour and contrast

- The photo can be cut to a new shape to change its composition.

- The camera disc can be cleared and reused after the images have been saved.

- There are no additional costs other than initial costs for the hardware, the camera discs and for camera batteries. Note that batteries do not last long when using a digital camera. The discs can be wiped clear and reused once they have been downloaded.

- Some digital cameras have their own memory chip instead of using a disc.

Some can take images that work as short animations.

- Digital cameras are available at prices that are comparable to those of good quality cameras.

4.3.4 Saving photos

Digital photos can take a large amount of a computer's file storage space. There are however, several ways that photos can be saved, some of which avoid this problem.

- Photos can be saved directly onto a hard drive. This would rapidly fill the hard drive space if saved in BMP format. One photo of good quality can take about 300 Kbs.

- An alternative is to have the photos put onto a CD using a CD 'burner' (copier) then to run the CD when needed.

- Smaller banks of photos can be saved on floppy discs.

- The number of photos that can be saved on a disc depends on the format used to save the photo. Photos saved in a compressed JPEG format take far less disc space than photos saved as BMPs. A JPEG photo of reasonable quality takes about 50 Kbs of space compared to about 300 for a BMP of similar quality. Other compressed formats are also available.

- Most drawing programs accept JPEG format images, though Paintbrush does

Annotating a digital image in MS Word

not. Most processors such as Word 6 also do not accept JPEG format images. This however, is likely to change with more recent products.

- A file can take less disc space if they are compressed using a zip facility.

4.4 Pupil activities in geography

The following list suggests some typical activities that pupils can do when working with photos on screen;

- to research or record information
- to add labels or annotate
- to change features
- to present information

4.4.1 To research or record information

Photos may form part of an enquiry or study of a place or geographical topic.

- A selection of photos can be researched from a wide range of sources and copied in several ways.
- Photos for field study enquiry work can be captured in digital form, as prints or as 35 mm transparencies. All types of image can be changed to digital form for use on a computer.

4.4.2 To add labels or annotate

Annotation or labelling can help highlight key features of a landscape.

- Photos imported into a drawing program can be labelled or annotated by printing text on the screen.
- Text can be moved to appropriate places either over or around the photo. Lines or arrows can be drawn to identify specific features.

4.4.3 To change features

Features in a photo can be changed to help answer questions about a past or future landscape, or sometimes simply to improve their quality.

- A photo can be enhanced by adjusting contrast, colour and definition, or by adding lines to highlight specific features.
- New roads and buildings can be drawn over vertical air photos as part of a planning exercise. New landscapes can be created. Past landscapes can be recreated.
- Layers of text or drawings created by a user can be stored or printed separately on some programs. Line drawings of photos and outline base maps can be made in this way.

4.4.4 To present information

Pupils' work can be illustrated by using photos.

- For hard copy work, photos can be copied and pasted into other documents such as a word processor program.
- Pupils can make a photo trail either as part of a wordprocessed document or a multi-media authoring program.
- Photos can be sent in digital form to pupils in any other part of the world on an Internet link.

4.5 Conclusions

The potential for using photos on a computer screen is enormous. There are some limitations for reasons of hardware and software capabilities and their costs. However, these limitations are rapidly being overcome. Increasingly, the only limitations will be the those of the creativity and willingness of staff and pupils to use facilities that are available.

Sample activity; landform processes

1 The aim of this activity is to show a landform and to give some possible reasons for its shape. It could be a landform that has been produced by erosion or deposition. The processes may be from the past, or they may still be active.

   a) Find a photo that shows the landform you have chosen. This could be from a CD-ROM, or scanned from a photo in a book.

   b) Copy and paste the photo into a drawing program.

   c) Type labels to show the main features of the landform.
   Research information, or make estimates of its measurements. Add the figures to the photo.
   Move the labels to suitable places on the photo, or use lines to point to these suitable places.

2 Put a copy of the original photo into a new file.

   a) Change the photo to show what you think it will look like in the future.
   Add labels to show what has happened.

   b) Make a third copy of the original photo.
   Change it to show what it might have looked like in the past. Add labels to show its features.

3 Use CDs and other reference sources to find out about the processes that may have shaped the landform.
   Describe and explain these processes in a word processed document.

4 You could import the photo into a word processor document then use the drawing tools to manipulate it. The drawing tools in Word for example, can be used to make a line drawing of the photo. The original photo can then be highlighted and deleted, or moved to a new position. This will leave a blank line drawing that you can use to show the landform's shape more clearly, without looking at other features such as fields and settlements.

Sample activity; local area study

1 This activity is to study the geography of the area immediately around your school

   a) Use a digital camera to take a photo of the scene outside your classroom window.
Make sure it shows something of the landscape outside the school.
As an alternative, take a photo print and use a scanner to change it into a digital image. Save the image as a file.
You could take a panorama of images that could be put together as a slide show.

   b) Open the image in a drawing or photo processing program. Put it in a square or rectangle, leaving some white space around it.

   c) Add labels to the photo by typing then moving the labels to a suitable position.
You could make a line drawing of the main features and land use by using drawing tools.

2 Write some notes in a wordprocessor about the photo to give details of;
- the name of street, district or local area shown in the photo
- where the area is, e.g. in which town or country area
- the direction it is facing
- the main types of land use that can be seen, e.g. housing, industry, communications
- the quality of the environment and what it is like to live there
- details of any planning issues in the area.

3 See if you can make contact with pupils who study geography in a school in a completely different part of the country, or in another country. You may be able to do this through a school Internet web site.

   a) Email your image to pupils in another school. You can send the image as an attached file. Send your notes as part of the Email.

   b) get an image back from the other school to show the scene outside their classroom window.

   c) Study the image you get back.
Make two lists, one to describe ways that the scene is similar, and one to describe how the scenes are different.
For a person of your age, what do you think are the advantages and disadvantages of living in each area? What other questions would you need to ask about the area? The other pupils may be able to answer them for you.

Geography through your classroom window

This idea has been adapted from an idea by Rex Walford for use during Geography Action Week. 'Teaching Geography' April 1998.

5 Finding out

5.1 Access to information

Computers have the potential to give teachers and pupils easy access to a vast amount of data and information. CD-ROMs and the Internet are able to provide much of this information. This chapter concentrates on the use of CD-ROMs and other software. Further ideas relating to using the Internet are provided in Chapter 9.

Access to information on computers has the potential to affect every aspect of teaching and learning, not only in geography but in all subjects. Skills for researching and selecting what is relevant are needed to take advantage of this potential. The full extent of these effects need to be seen as a whole rather than in the isolation of this chapter.

5.2 Types of programs

Programs whose main aim is to provide data and information have features that relate to;

- their subject content
- the degree of user interaction
- the program's platform

- the type and variety of resources
- the type of disc

5.2.1 Subject content

Programs with the greatest potential for use as sources to research information for geography, whether CD-ROMs or on floppy discs, are;

- electronic atlases
- generic information programs, e.g. encyclopaedias or newspapers
- programs with subject-specific information e.g. on topics such as settlements or physical features
- multi-purpose content, e.g. programs with topic overlaps such as between geography and science or another subject.
- photobase programs.

5.2.2 Type of resources

Programs that mainly provide information are different in the type of resources they use to present the information. This ranges between programs that contain only text, through to full multi-media programs with text, photos, sound, animation and video. The variety of resources affects whether a program can be run efficiently on a network, or whether it is best run on a stand-alone computer. As a generalisation, full multi-media programs are best run on a high specification stand-alone computer with enough memory, speed and other capabilities to cope with the amount and variety of data it is

Key words

♦ floppy disc; a disc to store computer data that uses the computer's 'a' drive.

♦ WIMP; Windows, icons, mouse and pointers

♦ DOS; Disc Operating System, a program that tells the computer how to work

♦ retrieval engine; part of a CD's program loaded onto a hard drive as an exe. file that allows the program to be run directly from the CD

♦ initialise; to load the retrieval engine of a CD onto a computer's hard drive

expected to process. More basic programs can be networked efficiently to 20 or more computers at once. Much however, also depends on the quality of the cables that link the computers.

5.2.3 Degree of interaction

The degree of pupil interaction with a program can vary between;

- reading and taking notes using a word processor, or copying and pasting sections of selected text or illustrations
- short on-screen activities such as using hotspots, drag and drop exercises and simple questions with a right or wrong response
- a tightly structured learning program
- complex simulations that involve decision taking and consequences.

Teachers should consider the value of these different types of activities in the context of contributing to a student's wider ICT capabilities, as well as to their own subject. Some for example, may feel

that a program that is little more than an electronic book is useful for little more than collecting information for their own subject. At a basic level however, comparing the use of a computer to a book is itself a useful lesson. Even basic procedures to load a program, scroll through screens and have immediate access to information can play a part in the development of a pupil's ICT skills.

5.2.4 Type of disc

It is useful to be aware of the different types of discs and the amount of data they can store.

- Floppy discs can contain a large amount of text, but a very small amount of other types of resources such as photos or other illustrations, especially if saved in BMP format.
- A program can be put onto several floppy discs, but these need to be saved on the computer's hard drive for the whole program to be run.
- CD-ROM's can contain vast amounts of data with full multi-media capability. These however, need a CD-ROM drive or the ability to run them to work stations on a network. The program's retrieval engine can be loaded to make access quick and easy. Loading a multi-media CD onto a hard drive is seldom a realistic option because of the amount of hard drive space they use.

5.2.5 Platforms for programs

Programs are designed to run on different operating systems (platforms), for example on PCs or Apple. Programs on a PC can also be written to either run in a Windows environment, or from DOS. The Windows environment is also known as 'WIMP' meaning windows, icons, mouse and pointers.

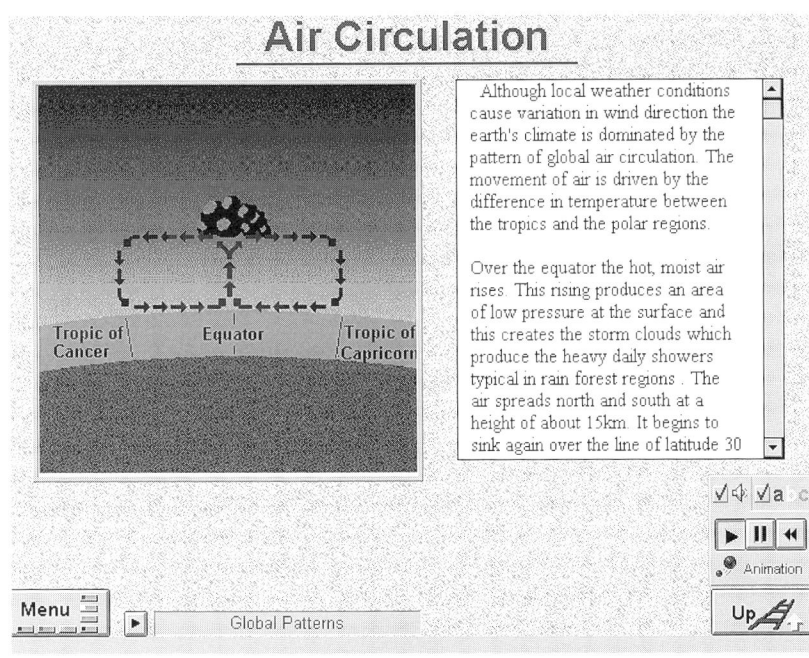

Weather and Climate CD-ROM, giving information with text, sound and animation, Matrix Multi Media

5.3 Running programs

Each CD-ROM has its own features such as its screen design, operating icons and navigation through its contents. They also have their own functions and range of media. Programs that are part of a set from one publisher, usually share some common features. This variety can create enormous problems because of the time it can take for the user to become familiar with how to operate them. Help files are usually available though the extent to which they provide help is sometimes debatable. Finding the basic common features is one solution to coping with this variety.

Programs have several features that are useful to understand;

■ amount and variety of resources
■ the toolbars
■ networking
■ quality and reliability of data
■ interaction

5.3.1 Amount and variety of resources

The type and extent of resources on a program is limited by the type of disc being used. A limited amount of data on a floppy disc need not be a problem on a program with a narrow focus and with limited aims. By contrast, a CD–ROM can contain a vast amount of data in different forms though many CDs use far less space than their actual storage space. Some contain far more data than the user may need.

■ The types of resources can include text, sound, illustrations, animations and video.
■ Text is best when written in relatively short line lengths and with a limited amount on the screen at one time. A scroll bar is used to read more. Some electronic books are available with little other than text. The ability to copy and paste text can be useful in these programs.
■ Sound can serve several purposes. One is to read written text that appears on the screen. This can help pupils who have reading problems or to help with the pronunciation of new words. Sounds such as language and music from other countries can help increase interest. They can also cause distraction to others if headphones are not used.

■ Photos, maps and diagrams provide visual information about features. The quality of illustrations varies greatly between programs, but can be excellent at their best.
■ Animations can be an effective way to show processes and patterns. Even a simple set of still frames can help show a sequence of events such as movement in the earth's plates or an erosion process.
■ Video clips are included in many CDs. Many of these are a poor substitute for a standard video player and monitor. They are often short, jerky and of little real educational value, though more recent programs run on high specification computers are of much better quality.

5.3.2 Quality and reliability

■ Questions are often raised about the quality and reliability of information obtained by using computers.
■ Programs produced by commercial publishers of programs are no different from books in terms of their quality and reliability.

Combining text with a spoken commentary on the European Ecosystems CD-ROM, Matrix Multi-Media

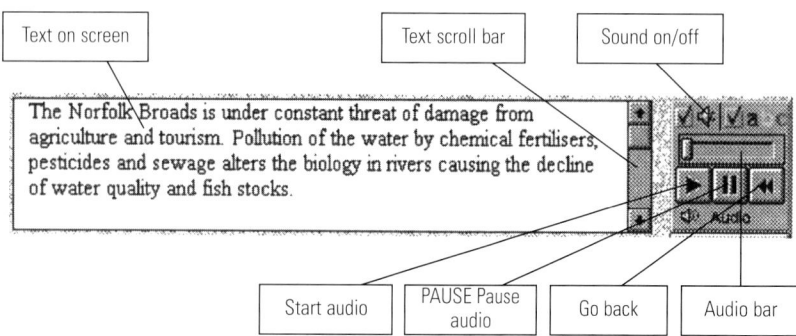

The Norfolk Broads is under constant threat of damage from agriculture and tourism. Pollution of the water by chemical fertilisers, pesticides and sewage alters the biology in rivers causing the decline of water quality and fish stocks.

Text on screen

Text scroll bar

Sound on/off

Start audio

PAUSE Pause audio

Go back

Audio bar

- Some CDs are available free from companies and foreign embassies. The usual caveats over bias apply to these resources, though they may still be very useful because of their bias.
- Using information from the Internet can be more problematic (see Chapter 9).
- There are special issues with regard to reading age, navigation through the contents and general ease of use where programs are used for purposes for which they were not intended. It can be tempting to make use of a CD-ROM for reasons other than the value of its educational input.

5.3.3 The toolbars

Toolbars give each program a set of functions that affect how the program can be used.

- Standard functions are often included on CD-ROMs, such as the ability to copy and paste text and illustrations from one program into another.
- A toolbox is sometimes provided to give a range of additional functions. These can include the ability to draw over images with a separate layer of data. Roads for example, can be drawn over maps or vertical air photos. Text or symbols can be superimposed on an image. A toolbox can also contain tools to measure distance and area.

- A magnify or zoom facility can bring up extra detail in a landscape. Interaction is created by moving around the photo using either a compass button, keyboard arrows or scroll bars.

5.3.4 Interaction

Some user interaction is possible when standard functions and additional tools are part of a program. Programs however, can also involve pupils in a wider range of decision-taking activities that involve using the data.

- Short multiple-choice questions are easy to tick and assess on screen. These can be part of a longer learning sequence.
- Drag and drop activities involve moving text or parts of diagrams around the screen. Text for example, can be matched with photos or moved to correct positions on a map.
- A simulation that responds to decisions puts the user in control of events, at least within the confines of the simulation's pre-determined rules. Pupils can make decisions on how to run a country's economy, a city's growth or running a farm. Random events can be built into how the computer responds to actions.
- Some programs aim to improve exam performance or to act as a complete learning program for a topic. These have value for individual work that involves limited learning outcomes.

5.3.5 Networking

The ways that pupils can access information on computers involves a high level of organisation on the part of the teacher. Much depends on technical aspects of the hardware and software. The Scheme of Work and lesson planning needed to use one or a few stand-alone multi-media computers, either in the classroom or in a central resource area, are clearly very different from working in an ICT room where there is full networking capability linked to about 20 work stations.

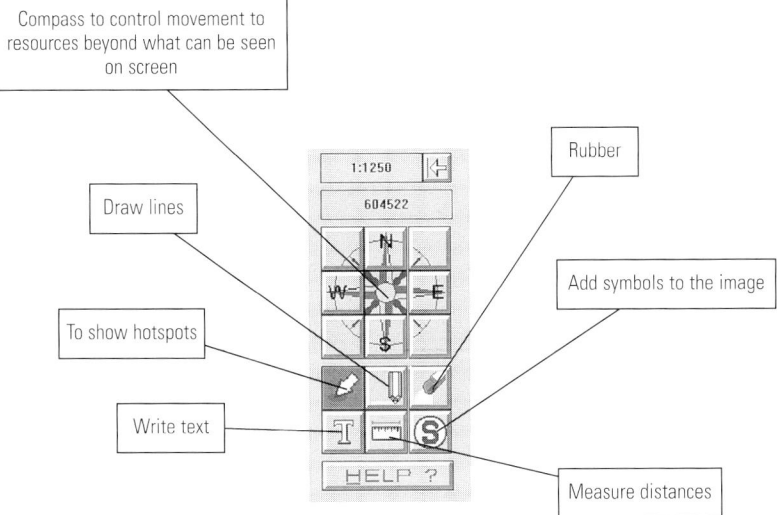

The toolbar in the York *CD-Rom*

5.4 Pupil work

Typical activities using a CD that pupils studying geography would do include;
- enquiry and research
- learning and test activities
- simulation and decision taking

5.4.1 Enquiry and research

Learning by enquiry can not be carried out without the resources to find answers to the questions. While some enquiries can be carried out using primary data, many can not. Enquiry questions that pupils themselves ask, are likely to require a far greater bank of resources than the geography department may have.

Using CD-ROMs and other ICT resources can help provide a solution to this problem.
- Different programs can be used to build up background information, for example, by using CD newspapers. Locations can be found using a CD atlas. Information about features and processes can be found by using CD encyclopaedias and other reference sources.
- All information however, needs to be selected and processed to avoid the dangers of copying sections direct from these sources.
- Teachers are advised to spend time in developing their pupils' research skills and where appropriate, to provide broad learning templates to give guidance and structure to their research.
- Pupils must be told to give credit to all sources and never to print off large amounts of text, especially when they have not even read it.

CD-ROM research strategy

The illustration shows how research using CD-ROMs and other software can be carried out in a way that integrates various applications of ICT. Other 'traditional' resources can also play a part.

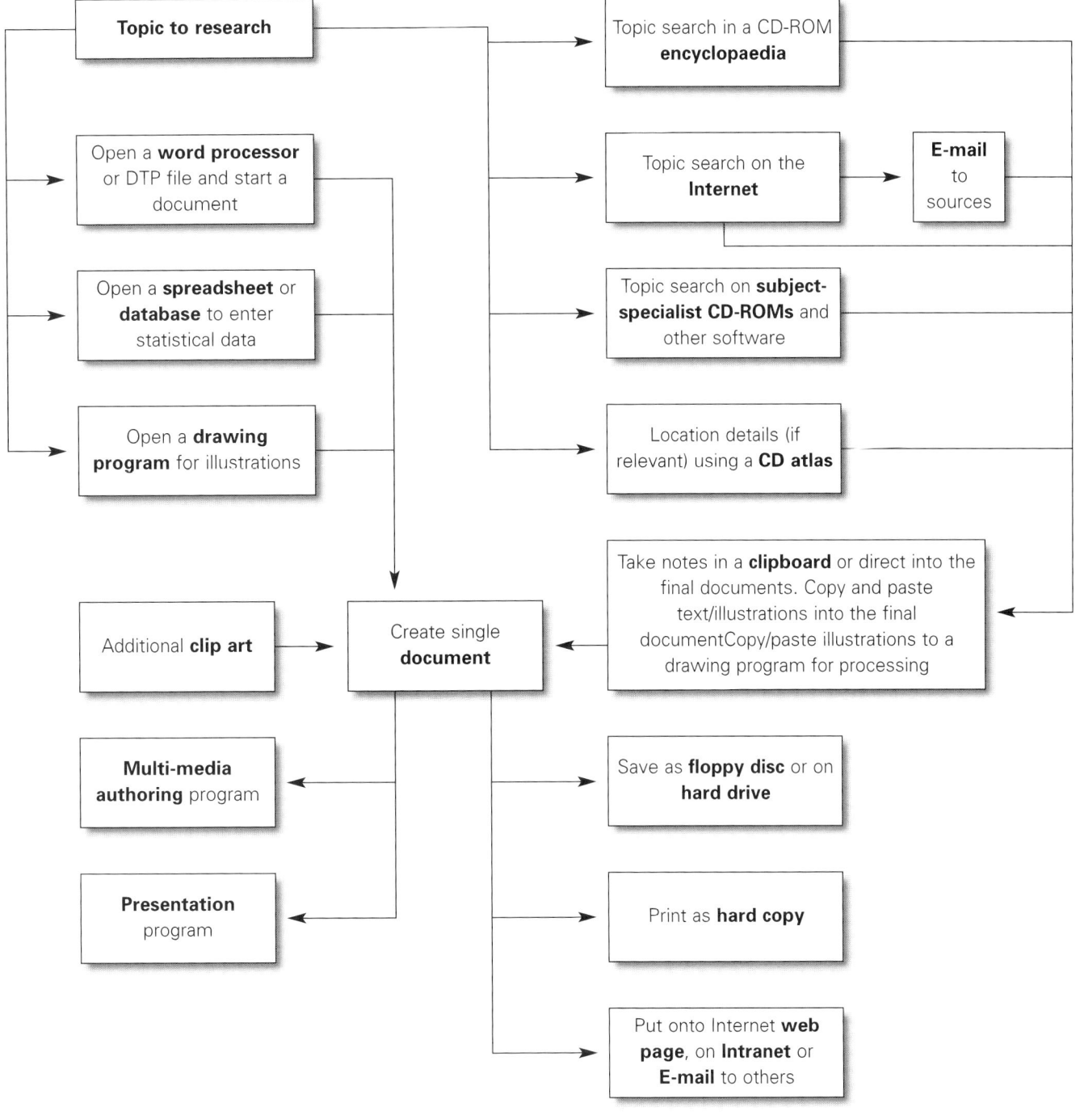

5.4.2 Learning and test activities

Some types of learning can be especially enhanced by the use of ICT.

- The different functions can be used to actively involve the user in studying and learning the material. Simple tests can provide a check that basic terms and processes have been understood. Pupils appreciate the immediate and private feed-back that tells them if they are 'right' or 'wrong'.
- A problem is that learning and assessment tends to be restricted to questions with relatively closed responses. Map and other learning drills such as multiple-choice questions are easy for a computer to handle. Assessing a well developed and reasoned argument can not be left to a computer.

5.4.3 Simulation and decision-taking

Simulations give opportunities to develop decision-taking skills.

- A computer simulation has the advantage of being able to carry out calculations quickly.
- A simulation can compress time to model long term processes.
- Reactions to complex sets of instructions and interactions are possible in a way that is difficult with hard copy resources.
- Although working with a computer is often seen as an individual activity, there is every advantage in using a computer as the focus for group work, using the computer as the means to carry out group decisions.

5.5 Conclusions

The rapidly expanding range of programs gives opportunities for an increasing choice of topics and learning approaches. There are however, technical questions about the capability of both hardware and software that need to be recognised so that the use of ICT can be effectively built into Schemes of Work and lesson plans.

Each program has both its advantages and its limitations. Although multi-media CD-ROMs have many attractions, it is easy to overlook programs with a more narrow focus, with more limited functions, but nevertheless with a value in their simplicity of operation and their ability to be networked.

Teaching the learning skills that pupils need to cope with the variety of programs, and the other skills needed to make use of their information, is an issue that needs to be addressed in each school. Taking advantage of the opportunities that increased pupil ownership of their learning can bring is a question both of the teacher's management style and educational philosophy.

Sample activity; levels of economic development

1 Carry out an investigation into the standard of living in one of the world's economically developing countries.

   a) Choose one of the economically developing countries in Africa, Asia or in South America.
   Name the country then use a CD-atlas to locate it on a world map.
   The world map can be copied from clip art, put into a drawing program then labelled.

   b) Draw a sketch map or import a clip art map to use as a base map of the country.

   c) On one or more maps, show the country's main settlements and other features of its land use and economy, for example, main farming regions, industrial areas and resources.
   Remember to add labels, a key, scale line and direction arrow.

2 Use a CD-ROM or other resources to research data about the people's standard of living.

   a) Find statistics such as the number of doctors per head, literacy rates and other indices you can find.
   Enter the figures in a table in a wordprocessed document.
   What do these figures tell you about people's standard of living?
   Find the same statistics for the UK. How do the figures compare?

   b) Find photos to show aspects of the people's way of life such as their homes, transport and types of work.
   What else do the photos tell you about people's standard of living?

3 Is there evidence from the resources you have studied that people's standard of living is either getting better or getting worse? Is this true for all or most of the people, or only for a few?

Sample activity; natural disasters

1 Choose a type of natural disaster such as a flood, hurricane, landslide, earthquake or erupting volcano. This could be one that is happening or one that is recent. Find out about it so that you could describe and explain it to an audience.

a) Use newspaper CDs to find out about similar events in other places in the recent past.
First write some questions that you think you should answer about the natural disaster. To do this, use these and other question words to start your questions; when, where, what, why, how.

b) Research background information about where the event you are studying is taking place. Use a CD atlas to do this.
Zoom in to see the greatest amount of detail. Details of the relief, climate, settlements and communications might be useful.

2 Find out from other CDs about what usually causes these kind of events.

a) Cut and paste photos, diagrams and selected text into a document.
Make sure to give the source of the items you have copied.

b) Use the information you have collected to answer the questions you have asked. Make suggestions as to where and how you could find answers to any of the questions you could not answer.

6 Drawing programs

6.1 Graphic skills in geography

Graphic skills such as drawing maps, graphs and diagrams are needed in geography to both present and help analyse data and information. Computer drawing programs can help produce every kind of drawing that geographers need, everything from simple freehand sketches to technical drawings such as block diagrams. Much of this work can be done using generic drawing programs. Specialist mapping programs are described in Chapter 8.

Paint and Paintbrush

◆ Paintbrush is a simple drawing program with limited functions, but with considerable potential if used creatively. It is part of the bundle of software on PCs with Windows 3.1.

◆ Paint is an upgrade version of Paintbrush. It has some useful additional functions, e.g. the ability to handle photos of better quality. It is part of the bundle of software on PCs with Windows '95 and more recent versions.

6.2 Drawing on screen

Drawing tools are available in four main ways;
- as the main tools in a drawing program or as tools in a generic program such as a word processor or spreadsheet
- an activity toolbox that is part of a program
- an animation program
- special purpose program

6.2.1 Drawings, maps and graphs

Most drawing programs are generic programs whose main function is to draw or process visual data. Some, such as Corel Draw, are part of a larger suite of programs. Others such as Paintbrush or Paint on PCs or Draw on Acorns are discrete programs.
- Drawing programs range in their complexity and functions. The most basic are generic programs such as Paintbrush and Paint. Others such as Paintshop Pro have many more functions.
- There is a set of drawing tools in some word processors such as in Claris Works and the later versions of MS Word. Similar tools are also in the Powerpoint presentation program.
- More specialist programs or sections of programs for special applications are available, such as for drawing charts or editing photos. There is a separate section on working with photos in Chapter 4.
- Graphs can be drawn from data on a spreadsheet. Further details of this are given in Chapter 3.
- Drawings made in a drawing program or spreadsheet can be copied or cut and pasted into another application. Some care needs to be taken to ensure that the file format of the image can be accepted by the other application.

6.2.2 An activity toolbox

A set of drawing and measuring tools is sometimes included as part of another program.

- The drawing tools can help make the program more interactive.
- The appearance of the toolbox can be specific to one program, though they all work in similar ways. There is for example, usually a freehand drawing tool, tools for drawing standard shapes and text tools.
- It may be possible to superimpose the drawings over a base image, creating a separate user layer. By deleting the base image, the user's own drawing can be left visible.
- Some tools can be especially useful for work in geography, such as a measuring tool for distance and area.

6.2.3 An animation program

Animation programs are a special type of drawing program. They are useful in geography to show how processes can operate over time, though the time to create them is likely to be a problem to all but the most dedicated.

- Short animations can be built up with a series of drawings, each showing a stage in the change. Changes in a meander bend for example, could be a

suitable process to illustrate in this way. This function may be part of a multimedia authoring program.

- Some more complex programs can morph between different images. This helps create a more even movement between images.

6.2.4 Special purpose drawings

Some programs are written to perform a particular job for a subject. In geography for example, a profile can be drawn using field study or other data using a program written for this purpose. Data is entered onto a table, then plotted automatically as a profile. This could show details of angles and land use along a slope, or measurements along a beach. The data can then be displayed graphically and statistically analysed.

In a similar program, river channel data can be entered on a table to produce long and cross profiles. Other calculations such as gradient, discharge and hydraulic radius can also be worked out and shown graphically.

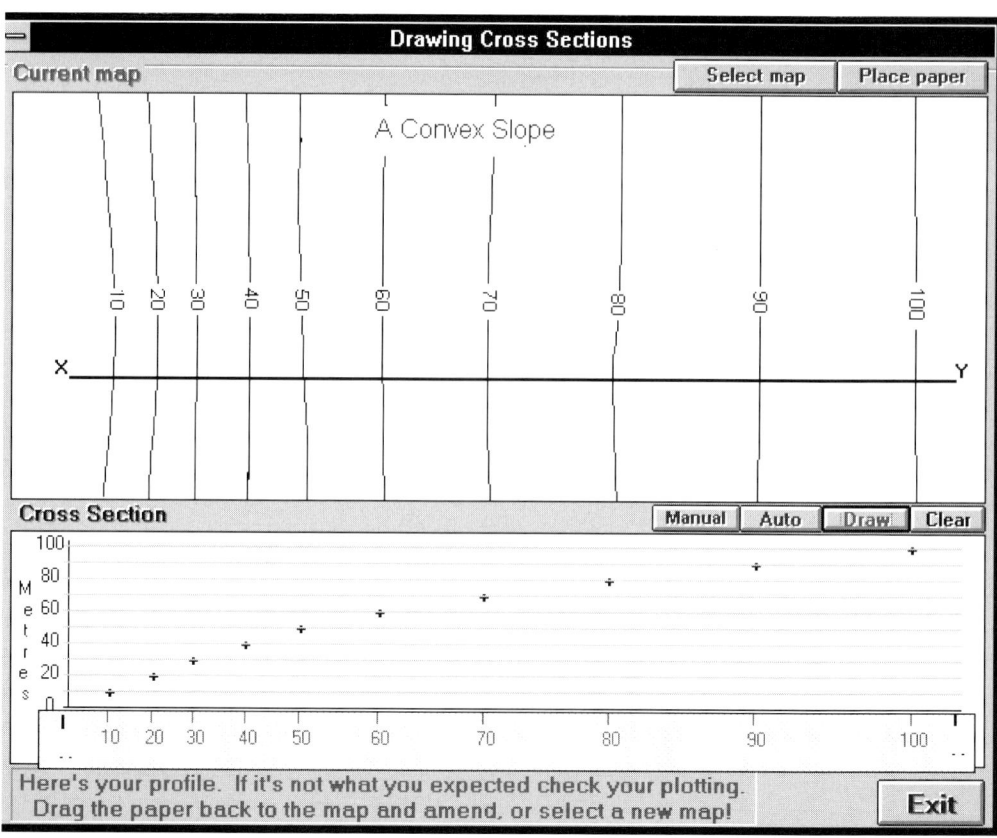

A program to make special drawings in geography, Mastering Mapwork

Key words

- ◆ cloning; to move colour from one part of the screen to another to get a perfect match

- ◆ graphics pad; a peripheral to simulate drawing by hand

- ◆ infill; solid block of colour inside an outlined shape

- ◆ palette; the selection of colours

- ◆ spray; a type of shading using dots

- ◆ toolbox; the bank of tools in a drawing program or other application

- ◆ tools; the different ways that shapes can be drawn or measured

- ◆ zoom; to enlarge part of the drawing

6.3 Using a drawing program

Three particular features of drawing programs and their tools have uses for the teaching and learning of geography;
- drawing lines and shapes
- banks of clip art
- the professional result

6.3.1 Drawing lines and shapes

Drawing tools are operated by using the mouse and pointer, sometimes together with a key such as *Ctrl*.
- Freehand sketching using a mouse needs practice for a satisfactory result. Poor results however, are easily removed and can be redrawn. A Zoom function can help improve accuracy and neatness by allowing detailed work to be carried out.
- Shapes such as squares, circles and ellipses can be drawn by dragging the shape from a starting point. These are useful for pupils who lack their own drawing equipment.
- Line thickness can be chosen, as well as the style of line for example, drawing continuous or dotted lines.

- Colours can be selected from a palette, either for the lines or to fill in shapes.
- Colouring tools can include an infill with a block of colour, a spray, gradations of colour, cloning colours, degrees of opaqueness or other variations. Most of these effects are difficult to achieve in any other way.
- Text can be printed in any position using a range of font styles, sizes and colours.
- Some programs contain functions to create special artistic effects. The user needs to find a sensible balance between the time to create these effects and the value of the end result.
- A graphics pad linked to the computer may help simulate drawing by hand in a way that is more satisfactory than using a mouse to control a drawing.

6.3.2 Clip art

Clip art is a drawing that has already been created and stored in a file.
- A library of clip art is provided as part of many drawing programs. Generic programs such as Word, Powerpoint and Claris Works also contain banks of clip art.
- Separate clip art programs can be bought. These contain items that can be used as map symbols, illustrations of places, features such as rivers, or as more general illustrations. Outlines of countries are easily available.
- Clip art can be put into a drawing program then changed to suit more specific needs. Maps with place names or quantitative data for example, can be drawn using a clip art outline as base maps.

Drawing tools in Paintbrush and Paintshop Pro.

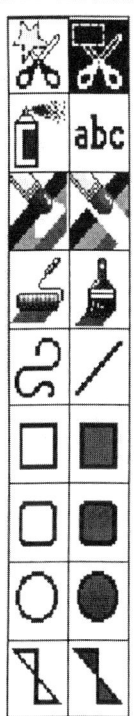

Drawing and other tools in Paintbrush

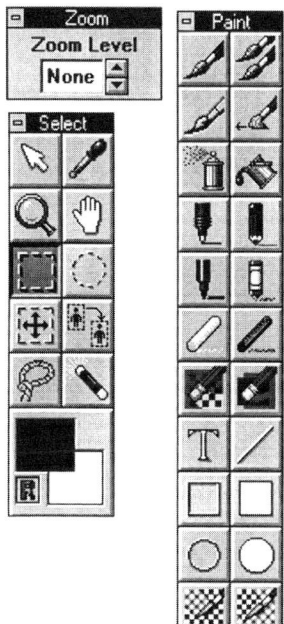

Drawing and other tools in Paintshop Pro

A clipart image (Graphic Works for Windows)

Features of a river valley

River cliff

Meander bend

Valley slopes

Flood plain

River channel

A diagram drawn in Paintbrush to show geographical features.

6.3.3 The professional result

Drawing programs can help pupils produce maps and diagrams that have a professional result that most pupils find hard to produce by freehand.

- Although some personal artistic flair may be lost, the result is one that can help improve motivation in an aspect of geography that many pupils find to be difficult, irrespective of their other abilities.

- There are questions to answer with regard to how work using ICT should be assessed. Outline maps from the same clip art will be identical. Map skills to colour and label neatly are not needed. The difference in graphics will depend on the kind of choices that are made over how to use the toolboxes and not on the quality of how the graphic has been drawn.

- A question can be asked as to the educational purpose in geography of continuing to teach traditional map and sketch drawing skills.

6.4 Using drawing programs in geography

Pupils can use drawing programs in geography for many purposes;
- sketches and other illustrations
- drawing maps
- changing features

More specialist programs are available for some of these applications such as for mapping. They may however, not be available or appropriate for reasons such as cost or complexity of use.

6.4.1 Sketches and text

The main purpose of most drawing programs is to create different types of sketches and other illustrations.

- Original drawings can be made using the drawing tools. These can be either simple line drawings such as the outline of a volcano, or more detailed block drawings with perspective.

- Labels or notes can be typed in any available space, then moved to an appropriate position on the drawing. Straight lines can be added to link text with features.

- Outlines can be drawn or imported from clip art by the teacher, adding labels if needed. The image can be saved in a *Read Only* format on a hard drive and used on a network by pupils. This allows pupils to draw on them but not to change the original. A simple activity can be for pupils to cut and drag a label to its correct position on a diagram. The result can then be printed.

- A drawing program can be used as a simple substitute for a desk top publishing system. A newspaper front

Importing a graph from a spreadsheet to draw a map (PCs).

◆ Type data into a spreadsheet such as Excel.

◆ Create a graph from the data, e.g. a multiple or divided bar graph.

◆ Make the graph a suitable size for the map you want to make then copy the graph.

◆ Open a new Paintbrush or Paint file.

◆ Draw or paste a map outline to the new Paintbrush or Paint file then move it to the bottom right of the screen.

◆ Paste the graph into the new file. It may import at a size that is either much larger or smaller than the size you need. You may need to either draw the graph to a different size on the spreadsheet, or change the size of the imported graph once it has been pasted into Paintbrush or Paint.

◆ Outline and drag parts of the graph to a place on the screen where you can tidy it up using the Zoom function and drawing tools.

◆ Then outline and drag the completed bars to the correct place on the outline map.

◆ Complete the map with a key. The original scale line for the graph can be used.

Importing a graph from a spreadsheet to draw a map (Acorn)

1 Open, or set up, your spreadsheet.

2 Create your graph.

3 Export your graph as a Draw file: menu (middle button) file save as Draw file (drag to your disc)

4 Open your Draw file: menu select select all; menu select group. (You must do this or when you put the graph into your map you won't be able to move it around.)

5 Open your map.

6 Drag the graph Draw file onto the map.

7 Select the graph Draw file onto the map.

8 Save.

page for example, can be created using combinations of text and illustrations. This can be done using a basic program such as Paint or Draw. An alternative is to write text in a word processor program then cut and paste it into a drawing program.

■ A brainstorm activity can be done in a drawing program by typing words on the screen. Once there, they can be moved to form sets of ideas. Doing this can help pupils to organize their ideas.

■ Links can be made by drawing boxes, circles or freeform shapes around words then linking them with arrows. This creates concept maps that show relationships between features. A similar activity can be done using Word by using the drawing tools.

■ Simple word activities such as matching 'heads' with 'tails' can be typed and saved in *Read Only* form. Pupils can then rearrange the phrases by outlining and dragging the 'tails' to match the 'heads'. Doing this however, would be an inefficient use of disc space as the file would take far more disc space than a wordprocessed file. Even continents can be moved using the basic cut and drag option.

6.5.2 Drawing maps using drawing programs

Generic drawing programs are one way to draw maps, though using a specialist map drawing program is likely to be more effective. In many schools however, using what is available may be the only option.

■ The most basic level of map drawing is to draw freehand outlines with shapes such as squares to show buildings. Colours can be added using an *Infill* function. Labels, a key, scale line and compass directions can be added using standard drawing tools.

■ Map outlines from clip art can be loaded then additional text, labels and shading can be added. Outlines can be saved on a hard drive as read only files then networked to be used by pupils.

■ Standard drawing tools can be used in geography to draw maps in a variety of creative ways. Boxes and circles can be used as symbols and to make dot maps. The copy and paste function can ensure that the symbols are to a common size.

■ The size of each symbol can be changed to make quantitative symbols. Line thickness can be changed to make scaled flow maps for example, to show the movement of imports and exports.

■ A map with located quantitative symbols can be produced by first entering data into a spreadsheet or database, then drawing a bar graph of the figures. The graph can be copied and pasted into a drawing program. Sections of the graph can be cut out and moved to particular locations on the map. This procedure is initially time-consuming but once mastered is a most effective way of creating maps that can be complex to draw by hand.

■ A simple activity using maps is to match country shapes with the correct country. This is done using a map with boundaries such as for countries or counties. Individual country or county shapes can be cut out and placed separately on the screen. These outlines can be outlined then dragged over the map until the correct shape is identified. Each country's name can then be found in an atlas and typed on the screen.

Drawing choropleth maps in Draw (Acorn)

1 Work out your key for the graded shading before you start on the computer.

2 Draw or import a map outline.

3 Create the key
- draw a box (box tool)
- select the box and, from the menu, copy it however many times you need to
- position the boxes
- select a box, choose style from the menu and choose fill colour; repeat this process for the other boxes
- use the text tool to label the key

4 Select a country, choose style from the menu and fill it with the appropriate colour.

5 Label your map.

6 Save your map.

Paint in Windows 98

The Paint drawing program in Windows 98 is able to accept and save images in the compressed JPEG format. Previous versions of Paint or Paintbrush are not able to do this.

Country	% in agriculture in 1993
Albania	46
Austria	5
Belgium	2
Bosnia	4
Croatia	17
Denmark	4
Finland	7
France	5
Germany	4
Greece	23
Iceland	6
Ireland	12
Italy	6
Macedonia	8
Netherlands	3
Norway	5
Portugal	14
Serbia	5
Slovenia	13
Spain	9
Sweden	3
Switzerland	4
UK	2

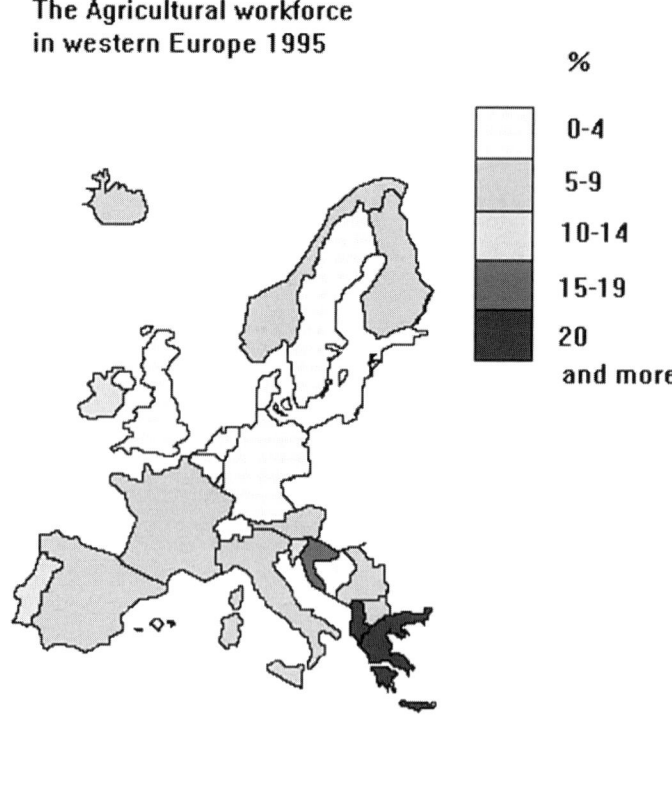

The Agricultural workforce in western Europe 1995

%
0-4
5-9
10-14
15-19
20 and more

A choropleth map drawn in Paintbrush, using an imported clip art outline and data imported from an Excel spreadsheet.

Population change in Italian cities

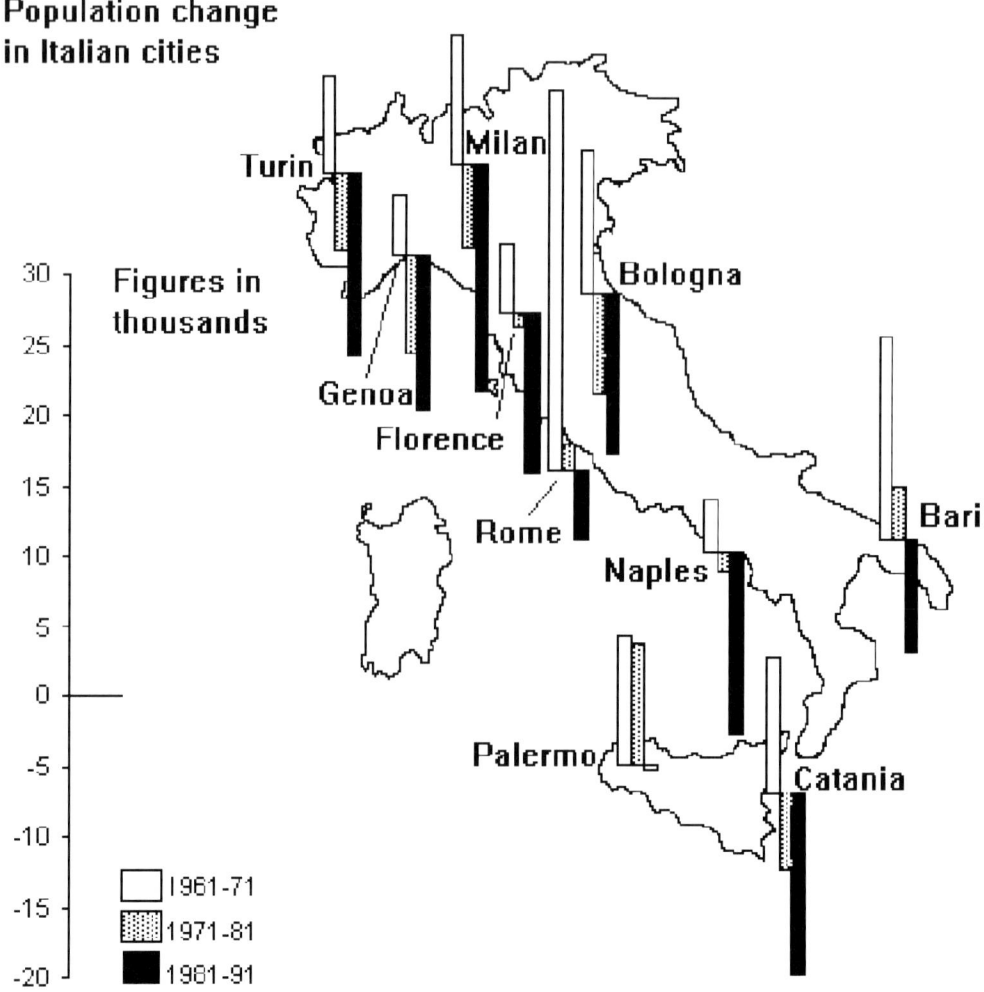

Figures in thousands

1961-71
1971-81
1981-91

A map of population change drawn in Paintbrush, using bars from a graph first drawn and then imported from an Excel spreadsheet.

6.5.3 Changing features

Features on a map, drawing or photo can be changed in a drawing program. This can help with decision-taking exercises, such as planning a new road or changing a landscape.

■ A base map or other image can be drawn or imported into the drawing program. Details of a proposal such as for a new road, can be drawn over a base map. Text, lines and outlines of different thickness and colours can

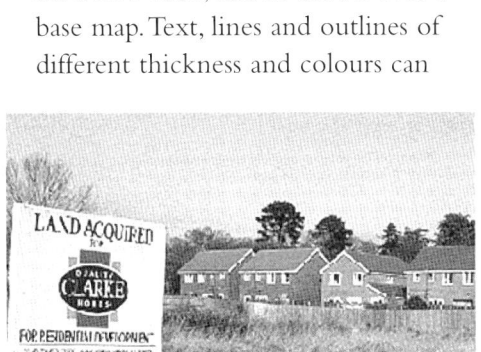

A digital photo or 35mm slide converted to digital form

Image after copying and pasting then editing a photo in Paint

highlight these proposals. This replaces the need for tracing paper, paper clips and coloured pens. Features that would be changed can then be identified and decisions made.

■ On some programs, the drawing layer can be shown and printed separately. Alternatively, if the base map is itself an editable object, it can be deleted leaving only the additional features that have been added.

■ Photos and other base maps can be changed by copying sections from another photo or map then placing it on the original. In some drawing programs, there are tools to clone one part of a photo onto another. This can be used to show what a valley might look like when covered with trees or if an industrial estate was built.

6.6 Conclusions

Drawing programs, including the most basic ones, have the potential to help pupils create accurate and professional maps and other diagrams. This is likely to bring gains in terms of pupil motivation. More complex drawing programs may also be used, provided that pupils gain sufficient experience with them to overcome their complexities. The problems relating to assessment however, need to be resolved. This can only be done by being clear about the criteria to be used for marking.

Sample activity; forests in Europe

1 Make a study of the percentage of forest land in the selected countries of Europe.

a) Find a clip art map of countries in Europe and import it into a drawing program as a base map.

b) Study the figures for the percentage of forest land in each country.
Use the figures to work out a colour coded key, divided into
no more than five categories.
It might help to rearrange the list in order so that countries can be grouped
together for the same colour.

c) Use the infill tool to colour in each country depending on its percentage of forest land.

2 Import the map you have drawn into a wordprocessed document.
Describe the pattern you have mapped.
What effects do you think that the amout of forest cover has on the geography of a country?
Think about;
- tourism and scenery
- wildlife and the environment
- industry
- river flow
- the climate.

Country	% of forest land
Albania	38
Austria	39
Belgium-Lux.	31
Denmark	10
Finland	76
France	27
Germany	30
Greece	20
Iceland	1
Ireland	5
Italy	23
Netherlands	10
Norway	27
Portugal	36
Spain	32
Sweden	68
Switzerland	32
United Kingdom	10

Pupil activity; environmental issues

1 Make a study of a local environmental issue in your local area. This could be a planning issue such as building a new road, a new supermarket, housing estate or leisure centre.

    a) Find and scan in or draw a base map for the area. .

    b) Add as much local detail as you think is needed, for example, roads, houses, rivers, main land use.
You may want to draw more than one map.

    c) Use a drawing tool to mark details of the proposed development on your map.

2 Now think about the ways that the new development would affect the people and the environment. You can do this using a word processor.
You can copy and paste your map into the document.

    a) Describe the different ways that the development would affect people and the environment.

    b) Do you think that the people would be mostly for or against the development?
Give reasons for your answer.

    c) Do you agree that the development should go ahead?
If you do not feel able to answer this, make a list of questions that you would first need answered before you could make a decision.
Suggest ways that you could find answers to these questions.

7 The weather report

7.1 Weather, climate and ICT

*W*eather and climate are topics that are studied at least to some extent by every pupil in every secondary school. They are topics that lend themselves particularly well to the use of ICT as it can involve so many different applications of ICT, including the use of sensors and other hardware for measurement. The use of ICT also takes advantage of characteristics of ICT such as speed, automatic functions, capacity and range. A module of work that integrates these different aspects is one way to demonstrate the effectiveness of ICT in the teaching and learning of geography. Opportunities for assessment are also likely to be considerable.

7.2 Weather and climate

Data and information about climate and the weather can be obtained in five main ways;
- primary measuring and recording
- data from satellites
- data from fax, phone, TV and radio
- the Internet
- CDs and other software

It is the first three of these that forms the main content of this chapter. The remaining two involve using aspects of ICT that are covered in chapters 5 and 9.

7.2.1 Measuring and recording

Weather data from the local area is easy to obtain using hand held instruments or from a school weather station.
- Sensors and other instruments can be used to take measurements of weather conditions in the local area, for example, in different parts of the school grounds. This data can be entered in a spreadsheet or database on a palmtop computer, then copied to a computer in the classroom.
- An automatic weather station can be fixed to one location in the school grounds. The site chosen needs to find a balance between one that gives useful readings, proximity to a computer and a place that is secure.
- Data collected by sensors is linked to a computer. The data can be either as real time data or a weather log can be built up over long periods, including over a summer holiday. The frequency of recordings can usually be set, for example to record every hour or longer.

■ A digital camera can be used to photograph the weather. This is especially useful to record clouds. A set of photos could also be taken to link wind strength against visible changes in the local environment.

■ Video clips taken using a digital video recorder can be linked to a computer by using a multi-media authoring program.

7.2.2 Data from satellites

Weather data can come directly from weather satellites in different ways.

■ A receiving dish can be linked to a computer to give direct access to weather maps and charts from one or more satellites. These are from both geostationary satellites in fixed positions over the equator and from polar orbiting satellites that scan smaller strips of the earth as they orbit the earth.

■ Receiving systems vary in their degree of sophistication and cost.

■ Previous weather can be played back to build up a sequence. Images can be saved or printed for further analysis.

■ Techniques of interpreting satellite images need to be taught so they can be properly understood. This involves developing an understanding of how images are captured in visible and in infra-red parts of the electro-magnetic spectrum. Using a combination of these images is necessary for their proper understanding.

7.2.3 Fax, phone, TV and radio

ICT includes electronic equipment other than the use of computers. These methods can be integrated with computers in ways that are increasingly easy to do.

■ Current synoptic charts, satellite images and other data can be obtained in the UK by Fax link with the Meteorological Office in Bracknell. The images and data are updated every six hours. Coverage is not restricted to the British Isles.

■ Information about local area weather can be obtained by phone to a local weather station.

■ Weather forecasts on TV and radio give national and local area weather information. Data for other places, especially holiday destinations, is available on Teletext.

7.2.4 The Internet

The Internet provides weather data in a variety of ways.

■ Satellite images both past and present can be viewed from several sources. The images however, may take some time to download. Some sources give free access requiring nothing more than registration.

■ Information about the weather in many parts of the world can also come from on-line newspapers and from other web sites.

A weather Fax from the Meteological Office

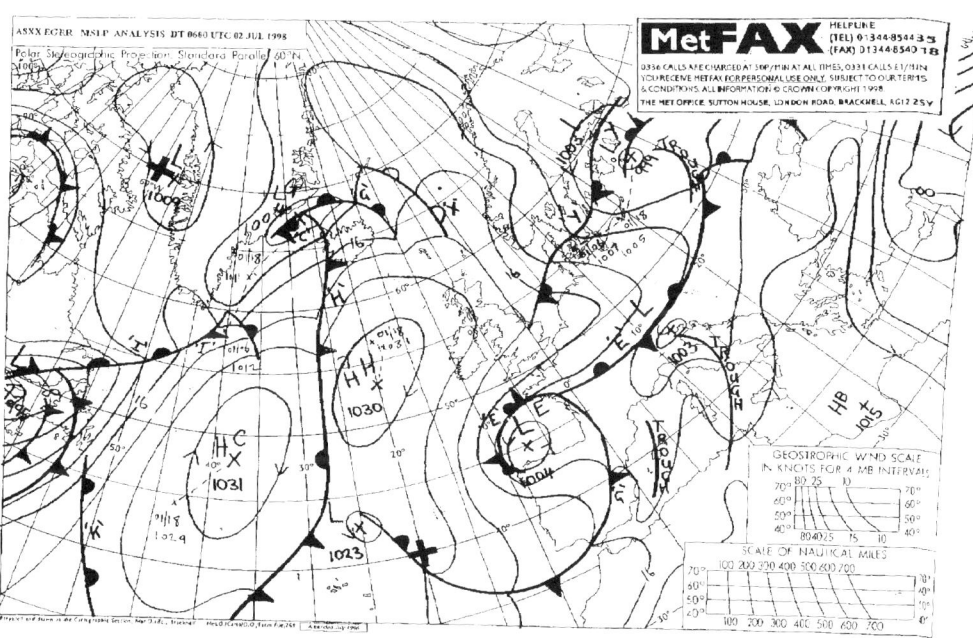

Satellite images

Satellite images of the weather can be obtained at no cost from the University of Dundee

http://www.sat.dundee/ac.uk/ and from the University of Nottingham at http://www.nottingham. ac. uk/pub/sat-images/meteosat.htm/html

- There is an international network of sites where digital photographs and live camcorder images are taken at regular intervals to show local weather.

7.2.5 CDs and other programs

Data and information about climate and the weather can be researched using the usual range of CD resources (see chapter 5) .

- Programs about aspects of physical geography or more specifically about the climate and weather, give useful background information about features and processes. Video clips, photos and statistics are usually included on multimedia CD-ROMs.

- Most CD atlases contain statistical data about the climate for each country.

- CD newspapers give information about specific events such as flooding and other weather hazards. Information about topics such as global warming and droughts can also be found.

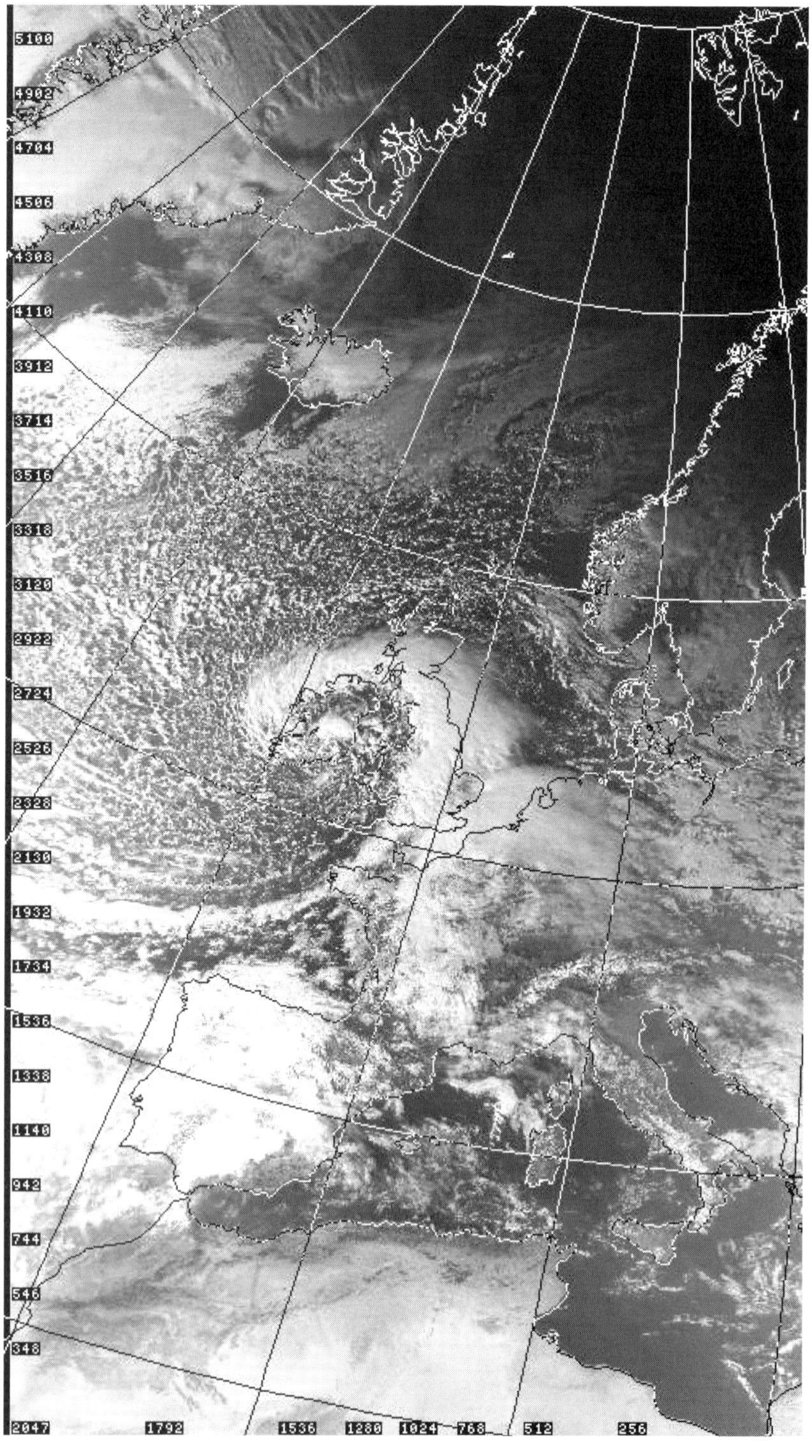

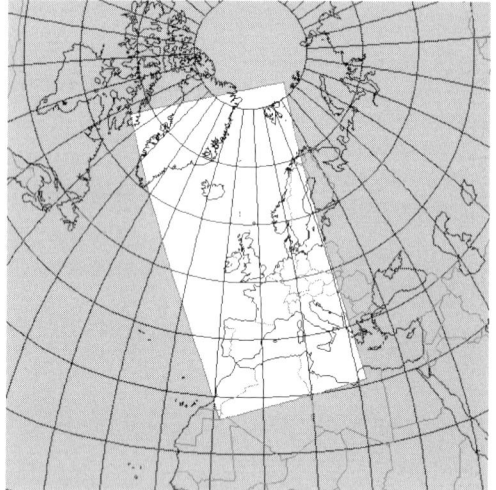

Weather satellite imagery
satellite map, area covered

Weather satellite imagery technical details

	Details of this satellite pass
Date	98-06-26
Satellite	NOAA 12
Direction	Southbound
Equator crossing time	06:44:04
Equator crossing angle	190.291 degrees west
Overhead time	07:18
Orbit number	36956
Identification	2199/10
Number of lines in pass	5484
Average altitude	833.250 km

An infrared image from a polar orbiting weather saellite showing the temperature and cloud pattern over western Europe for 26.06.98

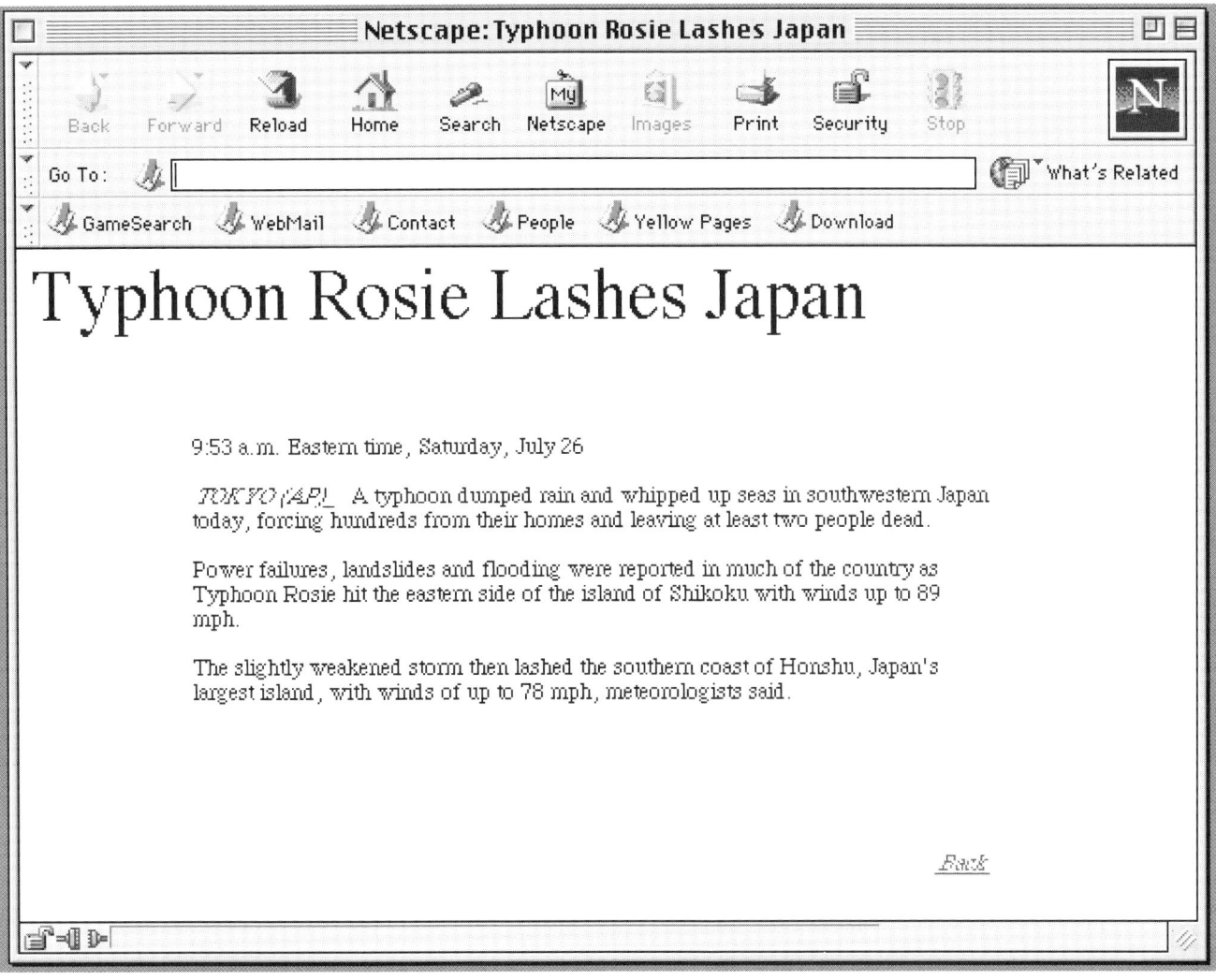

Typhoon Rosie Lashes Japan

9:53 a.m. Eastern time, Saturday, July 26

TOKYO (AP) A typhoon dumped rain and whipped up seas in southwestern Japan today, forcing hundreds from their homes and leaving at least two people dead.

Power failures, landslides and flooding were reported in much of the country as Typhoon Rosie hit the eastern side of the island of Shikoku with winds up to 89 mph.

The slightly weakened storm then lashed the southern coast of Honshu, Japan's largest island, with winds of up to 78 mph, meteorologists said.

Back

The Internet gives daily updates of data about hurricanes

7.3 Weather data in geography

Weather data can be used with pupils of every age in a variety of ways and using a variety of ICT skills.

- Raw data can be loaded into a spreadsheet or database for further analysis. This can include graphing work and statistical analysis. Weather records can be built up over several years. This data can be compared with local area weather forecasts to check on their accuracy or on local variations.
- A school or other local microclimate can be studied by taking measurements with sensors or other instruments. The results can be mapped on a base map using a mapping or generic drawing program.
- Information about a current disaster involving the weather can be obtained to become part of studying a topical issue or event
- Data can be exchanged with pupils in other schools either in the UK or abroad using Email or an Internet web site.
- Pupils can take responsibility for taking weather recordings then presenting the data as public information on a school notice board.
- Collaborative work can be done with other departments such as with science, maths and in information technology. This approach can help spread the cost of buying weather hardware and software.

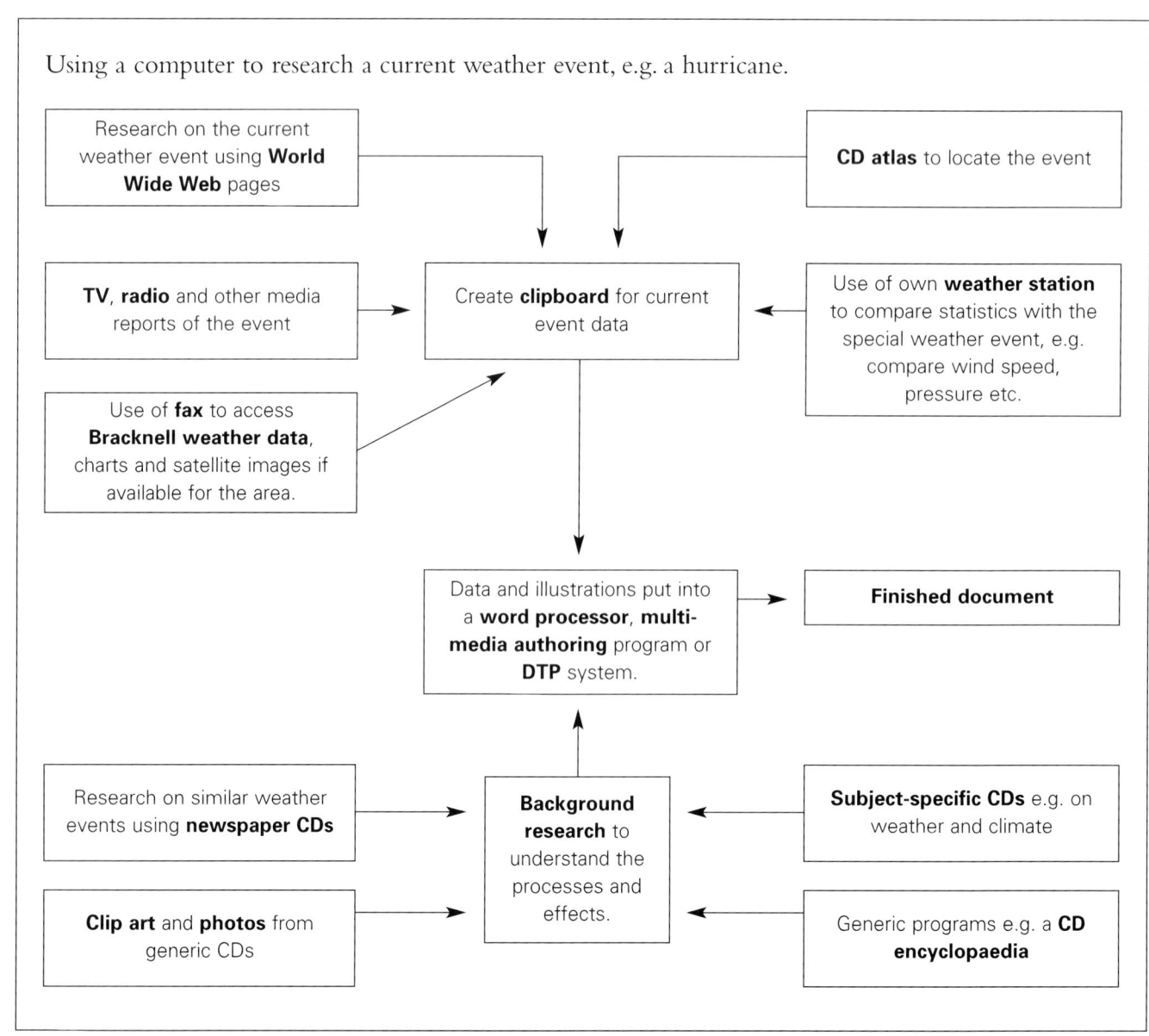

Using a computer to research a current weather event, e.g. a hurricane.

7.4 Conclusions

Work using all these methods is already taking place in schools. International links have been established, the Internet is being used and sophisticated satellite receiving equipment is already within school budgets. The use of ICT is certainly one way to generate a level of interest and motivation in what for many teachers and students, can be a topic that has been neglected in many schools in recent years.

Sample activity; weather disaster research

1 Carry out research into a present or recent tropical hurricane disaster

    a) Find out about the location of the hurricane. Use on-line newspapers on the Internet and other ICT sources such as television and fax to find out.

    b) Find its present and past locations using a CD atlas.
Mark its location on a base map. The map can be loaded from clip art or created from the atlas.

    c) Find out or make your own prediction about where the hurricane might go next.
What information can you find out about the area that might be affected?

2 Find out about the size, movement and weather features of the hurricane.

    a) Use the Internet or another source of satellite images to obtain a map or image of the hurricane.

    b) Find out about the effect it is having on people, property and the economy of the area.

3 Research the background to hurricanes using CDs and other reference sources.

    a) How do hurricanes form?

    b) What is the weather like inside a hurricane?

    c) What do previous hurricanes tell you about the kind of damage a hurricane can do?

    d) What can people do to protect themselves from the worst effects of the hurricane?

    e) What does the hurricane you are studying have in common with other hurricanes you have researched?
Are there any important differences?

Sample activity; tropical climate

1 Carry out a study of the climate in one location inside the Tropics (between latitudes 23 ½ north and 23 ½ south).

   a) Choose one location and find climatic statistics that give data about monthly temperature and rainfall. Use a CD atlas or other reference source to do this.

   b) Enter the data onto a spreadsheet.
Add the location's height above sea level.

   c) Use formulae to work out the rainfall total for the year and the mean monthly temperature.

   d) Draw one or more graphs to show the temperature and rainfall data. You will need to choose a suitable style of graph from the options.

2 Open a document in a word processor.

   a) Describe the main features of the climate for example;
- the average temperature
- total annual rainfall
- the temperature range (difference between maximum and minimum monthly means)
- the rainfall pattern
- how rainfall relates to temperature
- if there is a pattern of seasons.

   b) Research the other climates in tropical areas so that you can find out the name given to the type you have described, for example, equatorial, monsoon or others.

3 Use CD-ROMs and other resources to give an explanation for the climatic data.

   a) How is the climate likely to be affected by the height?

   b) What is the global pattern of winds and pressure systems in this area and how do these affect the climate?
You could draw and import one or more maps into your document to illustrate these patterns.

   c) How far is the location from a sea or oceans and how does this affect the climate?

   d) What other patterns and processes can you identify that affects the climate?

8 Maps and mapping

8.1 Maps, sensors and satellites

*M*aps are at the core of work in geography. Mapping multiple layers of data has developed into what is called a Geographic Information Systems (G.I.S.). Computers are playing an important part in developing the techniques needed to both create the maps and to analyse them. Satellite imagery is often used to replace maps or to help produce them. Data from satellites is usually captured in digital form by sensors, though photographs are also taken.

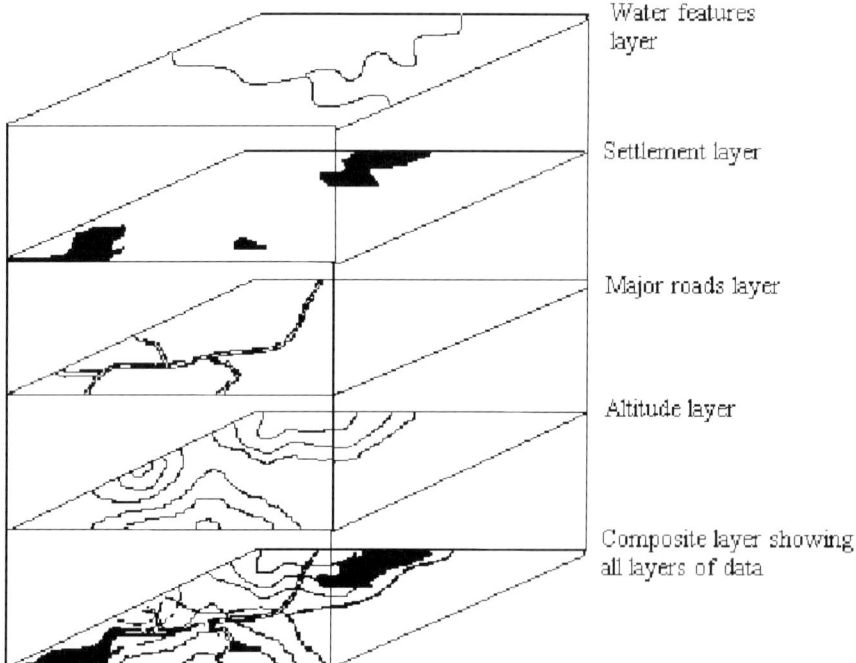

Water features layer

Settlement layer

Major roads layer

Altitude layer

Composite layer showing all layers of data

Layers of data that make a GIS

8.2 Mapping with ICT

Mapping programs whose main purpose is to allow the user to create maps from raw data, are now available for use in schools. These are different from the more general drawing programs that are described in Chapter 3. These mapping programs usually have a range of generic functions such as copy, paste and print. Of greater value are the functions that are more specific for mapping. These more specific features are the ability to;

- draw or import accurate base maps, including digital map data
- draw separate overlays of data
- map quantitative data
- question and analyse map data

Raster maps

- These are electronic pictures, usually obtained by scanning an original map

- The image can not be processed in any way, though it can be changed by drawing or adding data to it when the map is imported into a drawing program.

- The image loses quality when it is enlarged as each individual pixel is shown.

Vector maps

- These maps are made from co-ordinates that accurately plot points, lines and areas.

- The maps provide a good skeleton on which to build layers of data.

- Vector maps can be processed and changed in scale without losing quality.

- Statistical data can be linked to exact points on vector maps

8.2.1. Accurate base maps

There are different ways to create accurate base maps in mapping programs.

- Maps can be drawn by laying a transparent overlay on the computer screen and drawing beneath it using drawing tools controlled by the mouse button and cursor. An alternative approach is to draw on a graphics tablet that is linked to the computer. These methods are satisfactory for relatively simple maps where great accuracy is not required.

- Accurate maps can be drawn by using co-ordinates that are built into mapping programs. This allows lines, points and areas to be plotted with greater precision.

- Accurate base maps can be obtained by scanning an original map. Maps obtained in this way are simply pictures of the original. These are called raster images. They can be saved in BMP (bit map format) or other formats and imported into map drawing or generic drawing programs or a word processor. Maps, vertical air or oblique air photos can be copied and saved in this way.

- Base maps can be created from digital data as vector images. This enables them to be changed, for example by enlarging or reducing their size, without a loss in quality. The Ordnance Survey has agreements with Local Education Authorities and the GM sector to make these maps available to schools.

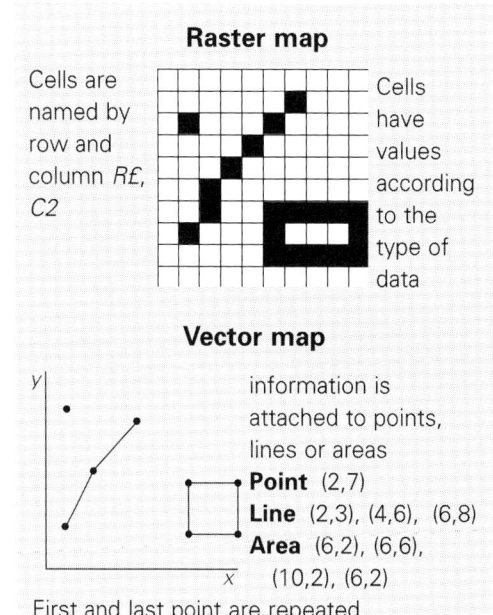

Raster map

Cells are named by row and column *R£, C2*

Cells have values according to the type of data

Vector map

information is attached to points, lines or areas

Point (2,7)
Line (2,3), (4,6), (6,8)
Area (6,2), (6,6), (10,2), (6,2)

First and last point are repeated

Features of raster and vector images

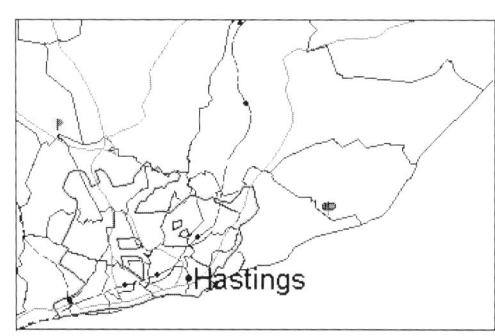

A vector map showing selected layers of data for the Hastings area

- Many generic programs provide clip art with map outlines, for example of countries, continents and of the world. These are easily copied and pasted into a map drawing program. Maps can also be copied and pasted from atlas

A vector map of Cornwall showing selected data, together with an enlarged map of part of the area showing layers of local area data,. drawn from the Scamp Census '91 program.

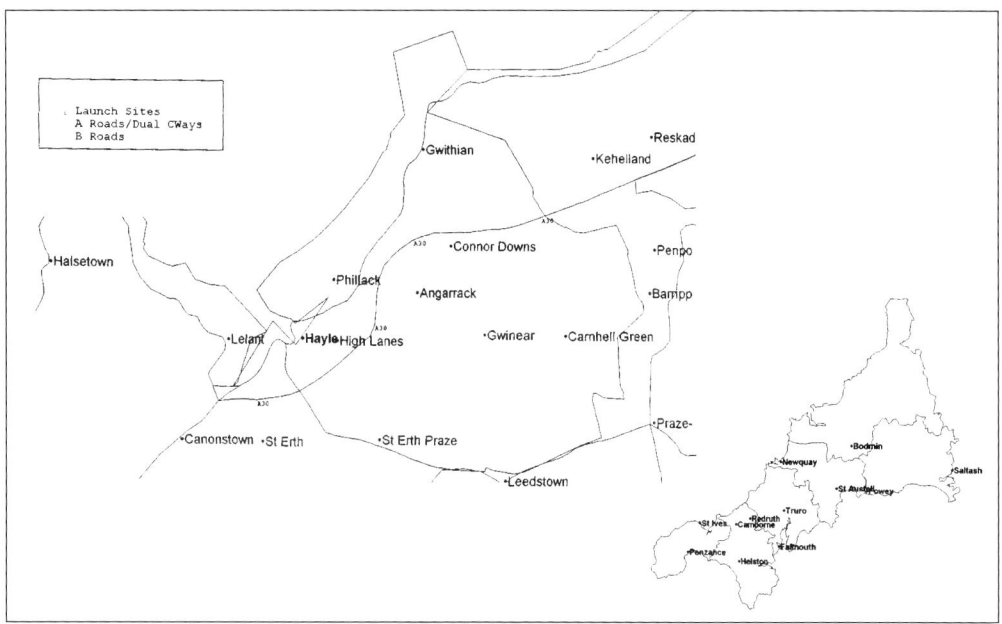

programs and many CD-ROM encyclopaedias.

- Base maps can be stretched, resized or given a different perspective using mapping programs and most generic drawing programs.
- Maps in vector form can be shown in 3-D when height data is loaded. The 3-D views can be repositioned to show different angles and elevations.
- Some programs, especially those with Census data, combine both a database and map outlines. Census data for the UK for example, can be mapped in a variety of ways and at a variety of scales.

8.2.2 Data overlays

Overlays of data can be drawn on base maps in mapping programs as separate layers.

- Mapping programs usually have a range of drawing tools to write labels, draw lines or symbols and to shade areas.
- Separate layers can be drawn with the ability to view one or more layer at a time. Layers that are not needed can be closed and hidden. Layers for example, can show relief, settlement and lines of communication, viewed either on their own or in combination.
- Each layer can be labelled with relevant information. The effect is similar to using sheets of tracing paper,

though it is more convenient and flexible to use and gives the usual more professional result.

8.2.3 Quantitative maps

Map drawing programs can visually represent quantitative data in every type of mapping technique, including many that would be too complex to draw in a school context using more traditional methods.

- Data for each point, line or area can be recorded on a spreadsheet. This can be either as part of the program or imported from a generic spreadsheet or database. The data can then be shown as located data in the form of a graph, a quantitative symbol or as different types of shading.
- The data range for different groups can be changed in the key, often with striking effects on what the pattern appears to show. The calculations needed to do this are part of the programs, requiring only a simple keyboard command to carry out the operation.
- Different types of symbols and different colours can be tried to see which is visually the most effective for whatever purpose the map is intended. The final version is then saved, but can be edited later if a different purpose is required.

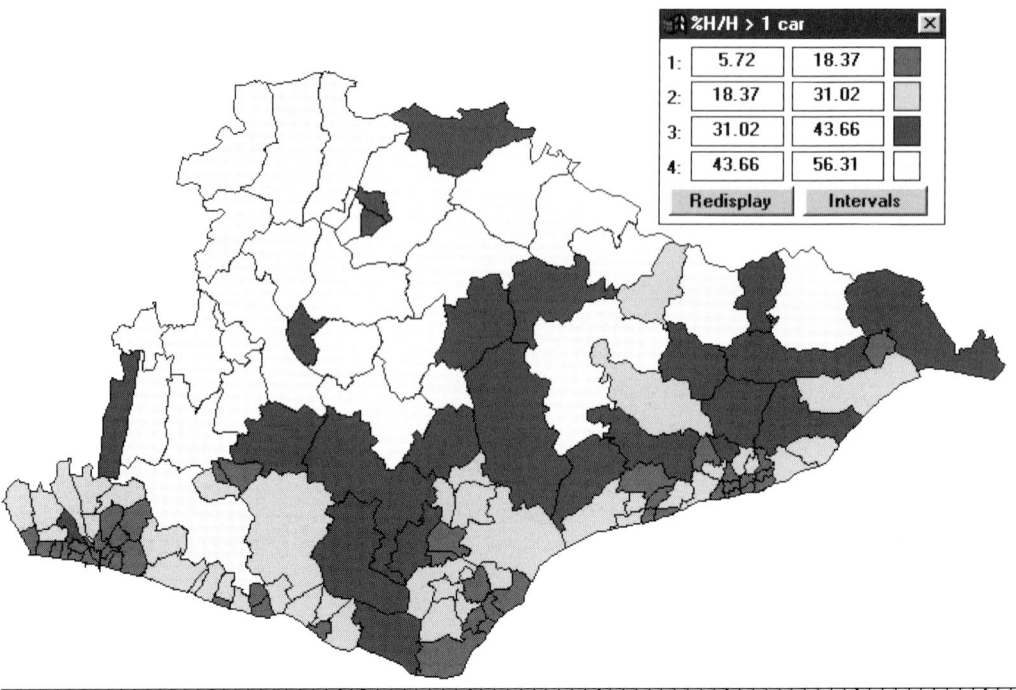

A chloropleth map drawn from a Census database in the Scamp Census '91 *program*

8.2.4   Query and analysis

Questions can be asked about map data, then processed for further analysis.

- Search and query functions are built into most mapping programs. This is possible when data is held in a database linked to the map. Data within a particular range of figures or for particular places for example, can be specified so that only that data is shown.

- Mapping programs can provide data about distances and areas on the map. This is done by providing measuring tools. Clicking on a start and finish point immediately gives a distance reading.

- Statistical tools can be used to process recorded data in the same way as data in spreadsheets and databases. Relationships between data sets can be found that might not be otherwise obvious, even when the data is displayed in map form.

8.3   ICT map work with pupils

Pupil activities with a mapping program can range from simple labelling of place names through to locating and showing complex data that can then be processed. The following items are some ideas that can be used or adapted.

- Draw a base map using clip art and add place names in correct locations.

- Create a base map of the school or local area using a scanned original map. Put the map into a mapping program to serve as a base map. Collect local data such as for vegetation, traffic or land use and draw the data on the base map.

- Using a vertical air photo or map, draw possible routes for a new road or a new housing estate. Draw further layers of data that is relevant. Analyse the effect of the alternative routes and locations on the area.

- Obtain a vector image map for an area you are studying. Enter statistical data on a spreadsheet, change the data to graph form and locate the graphs on the map. Describe and analyse the patterns shown on the map.

- Find the most visually effective way to show data that highlights the most serious areas for unemployment in a country. To do this, make choices over the style of map and the class boundaries of the data.

8.4   Learning about maps

Basic map skills is one of the few aspects of geography that lends itself to the tight approach to learning that is needed in a structured learning program. Some programs have been developed as an aid to learning these skills. They have some advantages in doing this.

- Mapwork answers that are either right or wrong, for example, if a grid reference is given correctly or incorrectly, can be recognised on a learning program.

- Simple animations can be used to show how to use grid references and other basic map reading skills.

- Short game activities can help explain then reinforce basic skills. Pupils can follow compass directions or answer questions based on a map.

- Photos can accompany maps in short descriptions of features and in quizzes. These can be ground views or extracts from vertical air views.

- A split screen facility can match up map views with a vertical air view in a way that makes reading the map and the air view more meaningful.

Key words

◆ drag and drop; to click on text or a feature, highlight it, then move it to a new position on the screen

◆ split screen; a computer screen that is divided in two to show two different images

◆ learning program; a program with information that is structured for the learner, usually containing tests for self-assessment

■ Distances and directions can be measured accurately using a measuring tool in a program's toolbox.
■ Drag and drop activities can match words with map symbols or other aspects of map reading.
■ Drawing tools can be used to draw contours and other features over a landscape where there are spot heights. Mistakes are easy to delete and change.
■ Cross sections can be drawn and in some programs, changed into 3-D images.

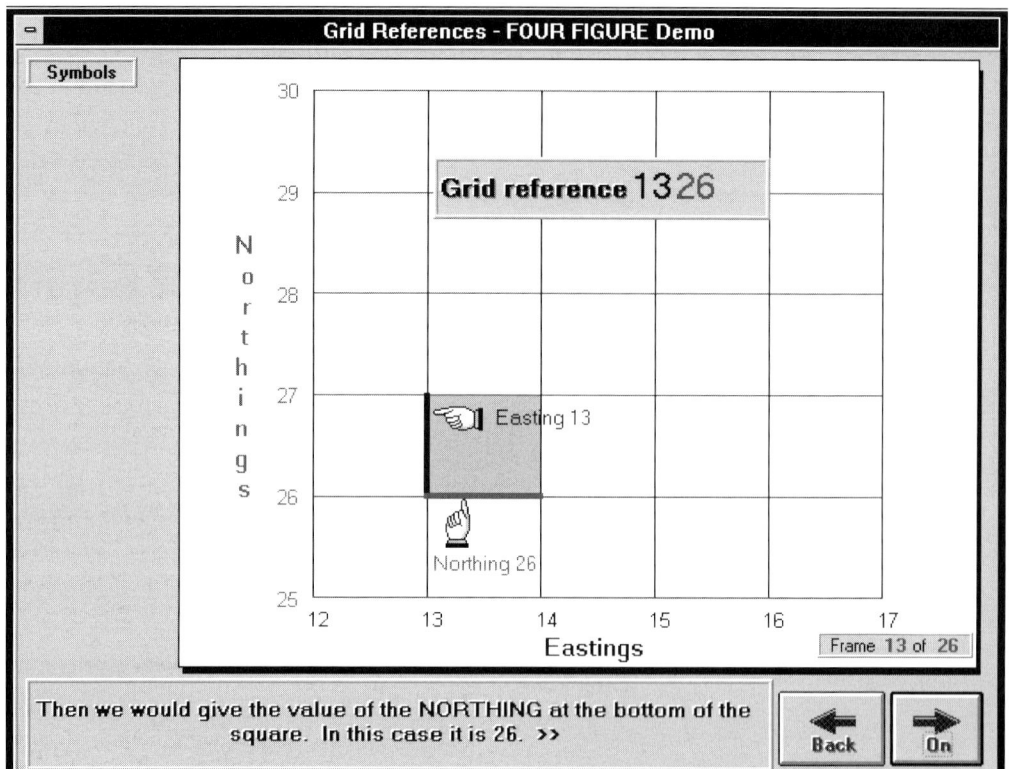

Use of simple animation to learn about grid references in Mastering Mapwork

8.5 Conclusions

Map drawing programs have great potential to help pupils present and analyse geographical data in ways that are both technically accurate and appropriate to the data involved. Maps are available in different formats, each with their own advantages and problems. Mapping programs are variable in their complexity though even the most complex programs have basic functions that require a minimal amount of practice to use effectively.

Sample activity; an environmental enquiry

1 Carry out an enquiry to show where the best place would be to locate some new litter bins around a school.

    a) Brainstorm a list of ideas to describe the ideal place where you think a litter bin ought to go. For example, think about places where people meet or buy food. Do this without thinking about particular places around your school. Write your list in a word processor.

    b) Now arrange the list in the order that you think these ideas would be the most important in your school.

    c) Draw or scan in a base map of the school.

2 Research relevant data for your enquiry.

    a) Identify by map reading and observation, where the places are that you need to survey, for example, the main routes and meeting points.

    b) Work out a shortlist of sites that you think might be suitable.

    c) Collect data at these sites to show the pattern of movements and other relevant data.

3 Display the relevant data.

    a) Map the data you have collected on the base map with located quantitative symbols or as flow lines.

    b) Use this data to check the best site against the list of ideas you have already set out.

    c) You could take digital photos of the different sites, then take a digital photo of a litter bin. Then import the image of a litter bin to the photos of the alternative locations you have selected. This will let you see what the new scene might look like.

4 Write a report using a word processor to describe your
- enquiry aim
- the methods you used,
- the meaning of the data you collected
- the reasons for your conclusions.

Sample activity; river field study

1 Carry out a field study to map a small section of a river.

a) Mark out and measure a base line where you have a good view of the area to be studied. Take readings to record the angles from each end of the base line to points in the landscape that can easily be identified, for example to trees or a river bend. Make sure you have cross bearings to the same points.

b) Use the data to plot accurate points using co-ordinates on a mapping program. Draw lines between the points to complete the map. Add a key, labels and notes to the map to identify the main landforms and processes.

2 Study the processes that are at work in the river.

a) Use a digital camera to take photos of features and processes.

b) Import the base map into a multi-media authoring program.

c) Create hidden or visible hotspots by drawing buttons over the places shown by the photos. These hotspots can launch the photo with notes and spoken commentary about each feature.

3 Use the map and photos to give a written account or a taped commentary of the features and the processes that produce them.

9 Using the Internet

9.1 A world wide network

Key words

- the Internet; a world wide network of computers

- Intranet; an internal Internet which runs on your own network.

- Web browser; the software that allows you to look at (browse) the Internet.

- Netscape Navigator and Netscape Explorer; two examples of systems that give access to the Internet web sites.

- Email; the electronic exchanging of mail via the Internet

- on-line; the time that you are working on the Internet using a live telephone connection or on ISDN line

- off-line; time that you are using downloaded information from the Internet

- download; to copy resources from an Internet site and save to a disc or hard drive.

The Internet is a world wide network of computers which allows access to a vast and constantly changing store of resources. Many of these resources can be used for the teaching and learning of geography. A problem however, is that the store of data and information is so vast that meaningful use can be difficult. This problem however, is more of a challenge than a deterrent.

This chapter examines the following aspects of using the Internet;
- methods of use
- finding and saving web sites
- connecting to the Internet
- using the Internet in geography

9.2 Methods of use

There are two main ways to use the Internet;
- on-line, using a live real time connection
- off-line, using data that has been saved earlier.

The most appropriate method depends on the aspect of geography that is being studied, the available technology and the costs incurred during use.

It is also useful to know that text and images can be copied from the Internet then put into another application such as a word processor. Text can be copied by highlighting then copying and pasting it. Images are copied by clicking on them with the right mouse button, then saving them as a file. They can then be imported to another application.

9.2.1 On-line

There are several features of using the Internet while on-line.
- On-line use is excellent when studying topical events such as the weather or natural hazards; some of the first pictures of the explosion of Raupai volcano were available on the Internet.

- On-line projects are constantly being developed for business, educational, scientific and for other reasons. One project on the Antarctic was created to allow children to pose questions to the scientists. Another (http://www. globalearn.org/) has involved pupils in following an expedition to Brazil with regular reports and investigations

- Pupils in one country can pose questions to 'experts' in another country about their subject.
- Pupils are able to gather reliable up to date information about weather conditions around the world from commercial weather stations. This can be done in partnership with pupils in other countries as a result of formal projects. Contact can also be made using the Internet.

- Direct links can be made to other web sites by using hot words, such as to the Encarta on-line encyclopaedia.
- A modem and software is needed to access the Internet when on-line. These are relatively inexpensive.
- Telephone connections are made at local telephone rates. This is in addition to the subscription cost to the Internet provider.

9.2.2 Off-line

For many schools, this may currently be where the potential for use is greatest. This is mainly for reasons of cost, time and to avoid the risk of web sites not being available.

- Off-line use gives the ability to download up to date articles and use them as resources that are either topical or as regular resources in the future.
- Downloaded information can be stored on a hard drive. The information can then be accessed by pupils at any time without the potential delays and restrictions of on-line use. Time saved for the pupil is however, at the expense of time spent by the teacher.

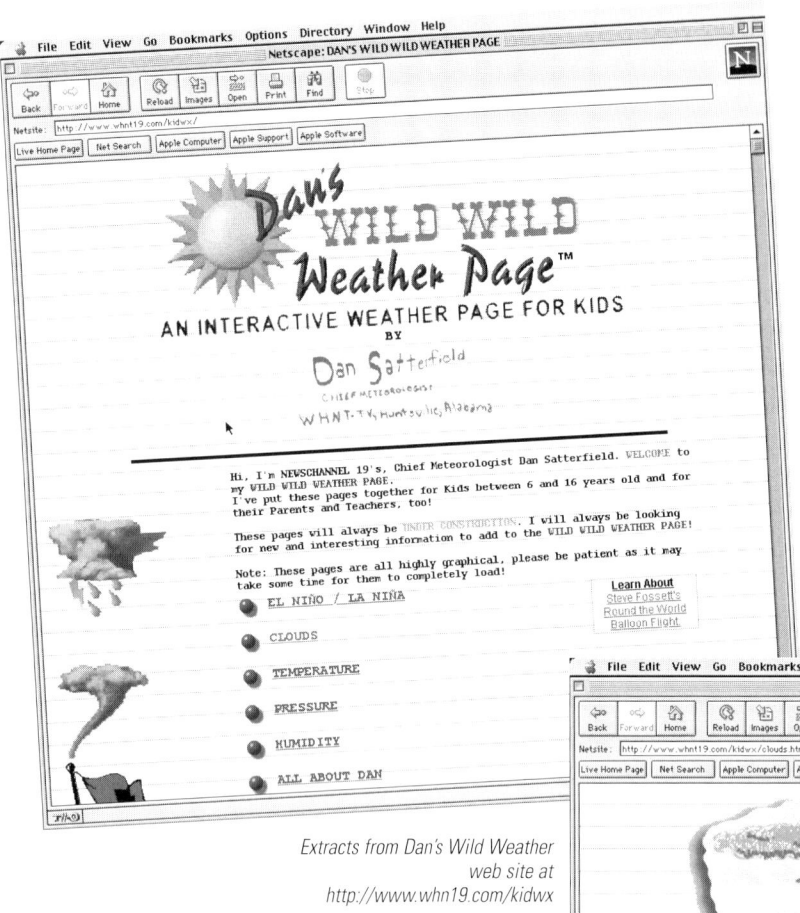

Extracts from Dan's Wild Weather web site at http://www.whn19.com/kidwx

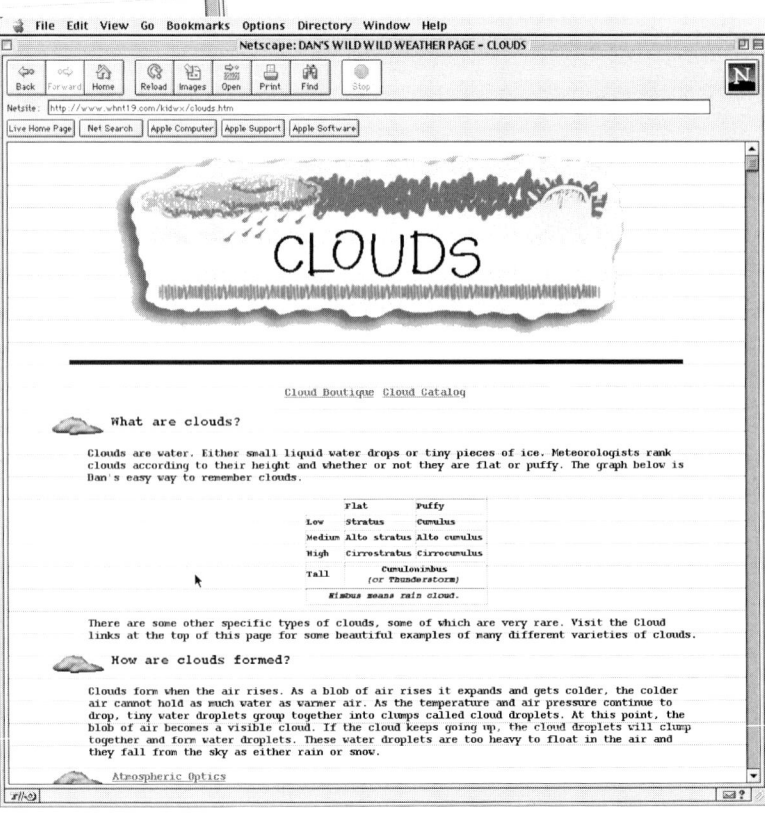

- Downloading information allows teachers the time to produce work sheet materials to utilize with the resource.
- Resources can be filtered by the teacher for suitability and relevance, though this approach can run counter to developing the pupil's own abilities to select what is relevant.
- There are no telephone call charges, except for when the data was originally researched and saved.

On-line and off-line: A summary of problems and solutions

Problems	Solutions
The high cost of on-line use using a telephone line	Try downloading information onto your hard drive or network server so you can use it off-line. Make out a case at whole-school level to install an ISDN line.
Finding sites and loading information seems slow after 11am	Use off-line instead of using live so you are not competing with other parts of the world, especially the USA. Install an ISDN line and more powerful computer.
Access to pornography	Your ICT co-ordinator should choose a service provider who operates a filter system. The RM 'Internet for Learning' is one of these. This is designed to keep out unwanted images, though it may not be entirely effective. Maintain vigilance while children are using the Internet.

9.2.3 An Intranet

An Intranet is a way of using the functions of the Internet, but in a way that can only be accessed by the school. Each department can set up its own area on the Intranet, making resources available, giving and exchanging information and for any other use they have. A school Intranet can extend to the pupils' homes and to a range of other local organisations. It can, and in some cases already has, become a means of communicating resources, homework and other materials not only inside the school, but within the local area.

9.2.4 Email

Email is a means of sending messages quickly, relatively cheaply, efficiently and with several other advantages.

- A message is typed either directly into the Email composition page, or it can be written in a word processor then copied and pasted.
- A file containing existing data can be attached to the message, for example a photo, a spreadsheet or a wordprocessed document. This can be launched by the receiver, provided the formats and systems are compatible. Worksheets and other geographical resources can be exchanged in this way.
- A mail list can be set up, listing the Email addresses all the people in a particular group with whom you want to make contact. This could be to all

the other geography teachers in a local area, members of the local Geographical Association or to other contacts you have. By using the list as the address, the same message can be sent to all members of the group by sending only one message.

■ Once the system has been set up, contact with pupils in other parts of the UK, or with pupils in other countries, involves little more than typing the message.

■ Email is a process that is quick and immediate to use. Messages sent on Email can have a better chance of a quick response than messages sent by mail or even by fax.

Web site terms

◆ http; hyper text transfer protocol, one of several ways that information is transfered between computers

◆ www; world wide web, a system of links for information and resources on the Internet

◆ org; a charitable organisation

◆ co; a company

◆ ac; an institution of Higher Education, university etc.

◆ uk; a web address the uk

◆ URL; uniform resource locator, the address of a web site

Search engines

Further information about using Search Tools is available on the BECTA web site at http://www.becta.org.uk/info-sheets/intsearch.html

9.3 Finding and saving web sites

Finding web sites involves either
■ using a search engine
■ getting information directly about a web site from another source.

Saving useful sites can also be done on screen by using a bookmark facility.

9.3.1 Search engines

Search engines are the electronic equivilant to using different encyclopedias to find information about a topic. The same or similar information may be there, but it has a different index, it is presented in a different way and is organized in a different structure.

■ There are about 300 different search engines though only a few are commonly used. Excite, Lycos and Infoseek are three of these. Users often develop a preference for one or other of the search engines.

■ All search engines work by looking for the subject, place or name that is typed in as a search entry. Some search engines such as Lycos use a computer to both record then find key words or phrases. Others such as Yahoo have been sorted into categories by people.

■ Each search engine runs off a different database so it is worthwhile trying more than one search engine for the same search word.

■ Some search engines attempt to rank the sites in order of relevance. The order of relevance however, may not match what is relevant to your particular needs. A phrase such as 'more like this' is sometimes shown to prompt the user to investigate more sites along a particular line of thought.

■ Precise questions in the form of combinations of search words need to be entered in order to give the most relevant sites. Pupils need to be trained to make use of the different codes that link words in the search for example, putting AND (in upper case) between words to link them or putting words in quotation marks. A single word entry on almost any topic can produce a list of millions of entries.

9.3.2 Direct sources for web sites

Web sites can be found by looking in several different types of source.

■ There are educational web sites such as BECTA and the Virtual Teachers' Centre.

■ Web sites are sometimes listed in published journals and periodicals such as 'Teaching Geography', 'Educational Computing', the TES and many others.

■ Some computer companies are developing their own bank of educational sites. These include sites identified by British Telecom on Campus World and Research Machines.

■ Many schools are independently building up their own bank of sites. These sites are saved as bookmarks for future use. Although these match the needs of individual schools, many are

Key web sites

◆ BECTA; http://www.becta.org.uk/index.html

BECTA geography resource links;
http://ultra1.ncet.org.uk/projects/cits/geog/index.html

◆ Geographical Association; http://WWW.GEOGRAPHY.ORG.UK/

◆ National Grid for Learning; http://vtc.ngfl.gov.uk/

◆ Virtual Teacher Centre; http://vtc.ngfl.gov.uk/vtc/index.html

◆ Newman College of Higher Education
http://www.newman.ac.uk/links.html

◆ RM service provider; http://www.rmplc.co.uk

Ten useful URLs for geography

Ten useful URLs for geography

Note that website addresses sometimes move. A message is sometimes given about the new address, but often not.

http://www.jin.org/Kidsweb

This site gives excellent information about Japan for KS 3 level students. It is well written and easy to follow.

http://www.oneworld.org/

A first rate site for 'A' level students. It contains a wealth of recent and relevant material for most parts of an 'A' level syllabus.

http://www.whnt19.com/kidwx/

A site for KS3 with information about weather including chances to Email the site and obtain lesson plans.

http://www.foe.co.uk/fund/welcome/about_foe.html

Friends of the Earth home page, a source of information on environmental issues and projects

http://volcano.und.nodak.edu/vwdocs/Online/index.html

A site that answers common questions about volcanoes, and leads to many other web sites with information and photos about volcanoes. Questions can be asked on Email. Lesson plans are also available.

http://www.ezinfo.ethz.ch/ezinfo/volcano/strombolihomee.html

The site provides the basis for a virtual fieldtrip to the summit of Stromboli. It is best if you download it and prepare worksheets for the students to take on the field trip. A similar virtual visit can be made up Mount Fuji in Japan.

http://www.geolsoc.org.uk/gs3etfrm.htm

The US Geological Survey website for education. This includes ideas for lessons and links to other web sites with earth science information.

http://uk5.multimap.com/map/places.cgi

An atlas of places in the UK, including daily weather information.

http://www.met.office.gov.uk

The Meteorological Office at Bracknell.

http://www.bbc.co.uk/education/cdb/index.shtml

The BBC education website. This gives access to help about using different applications of ICT. There is also revision material for GCSE pupils.

likely to be of use to others. Ways to share information about these web sites is needed.

■ Many sites are found by a combination of focused research and by accident. Words such as 'surfing', 'trawling' and 'grazing' are used to describe these processes. One site often leads to another, then to another. This can be either enormously productive, or disappointingly unproductive, with costs to match.

9.3.3 Saving sites

Useful web sites can be saved as a bookmark, also called favourites. This is done by clicking on the bookmark option when a web site page is on screen, then choosing Add bookmark. The bookmarks can be arranged in directories in much the same way as organising work in a file manager. The directories can be rearranged and edited at any time.

Emailing websites

A useful site can be sent to someone else by Email.

◆ Highlight the web site address when the site is on the screen, then click on Edit and copy.

◆ Open a new message in Email.

◆ Place the cursor in the text area, then click on Edit and paste.

◆ Complete the message and send it as normal.

◆ When the Email is opened, the web address appears in blue. By clicking on it, the Internet browser will open and the web site will be found. It can then be bookmarked by the receiver.

Sharing web sites

At Churchill school near Bristol, the geography department puts the URL for useful sites in the geography area of the school's web page. An E-mail can be sent to the site to see if there are lesson plans and other accompanying resources (http://www.rmplc.co.uk/eduweb/sites/churchil/index.html).

Key text

'A geographer's guide to the Internet', Karl Donert, The Geographical Association 1997

9.4 Connecting to the Internet

Getting connected to the Internet involves whole-school decisions. The connection can be either to a stand-alone computer, or preferably though at much greater cost but of far greater educational value, to be networked.

- Access involves issues relating to hardware and to internal cabeling for a network. A key decision is whether to use a telephone line connection or a special link called an ISDN (Integrated Services Digital Network) line. The decision may also involve a consideration of opportunities for video-conferencing.

- A telephone link has a low short term installation cost, but high longer term running costs. An ISDN line has a higher initial cost, but much lower running costs.

- The costs need to be justified in terms of the educational quality of its use. Geographers should be able to make out a strong case that this is a resource with enormous potential for raising educational standards both in geography and in other key areas of the curriculum such as in English, as well as in the pupils' understanding of ICT itself. The raising of standards however, may be more in terms of the quality of the geography rather than in changes to published examination grades. The two should not, but may be rather different.

9.5 Geographers on the Internet

The Internet is used for many different reasons, including education. For geography some reasons for its use are as follows.

- To access data and information from across the globe that distance or cost would otherwise make inaccessible

- To teach pupils the value of using several sources to gather information as part of their geographical enquiry skills.

- It allows pupils access via web pages to pupils in countries which have ideas and information based on viewpoints and values developed in different socio-economic contexts.

- The Internet gives up to date data to use, including information on topical events.

- There are pre-planned lessons on the Internet, some prepared by companies to further the use of their software and some by other teachers. You can add to this list by creating your own web page to share your good ideas and resources.

- Some sites give virtual tours of locations of interest to geography, for example a visit to the Stromboli or Mount Fuji volcanoes.

- To help develop skills of selection and to check for bias and accuracy. All Internet entries are not subject to scrutiny. Users need to be aware of this and make every effort to both understand the nature of the source, and to cross-check the information.

Lesson ideas from the US Geological Survey

Two more general reasons are also worth mentioning.

- As a way to improve a pupil's writing skills, a benefit that comes from spending time on-line writing school or personal web pages and Email where text must be written in a way that is clear, economical and can make use of a spell check.
- To develop generic ICT skills.

9.6 Conclusions

The Internet including Email has evolved and grown rapidly. Ideas about its educational value are in their relative infancy and there are certainly many technical, cost, planning and other problems associated with its use. It is however, a resource with enormous potential to facilitate the teaching and learning of geography. The challenge is to take advantage of these opportunities. Identifying and developing the skills that pupils and teachers need to use it effectively is a process that is only just starting.

Sample activity; weather forecasting

1 Find on a web site, such as on the Multimap site (http://uk5.multimap.com/map/places.cgi) or listen to a weather forecast on radio or television for the next day for the local area.

   a) Write down details of the forecast.

   b) Check the pattern of weather on the
       Internet by looking at satellite images or getting a fax from the national weather forecasting centre at Bracknell.

   c) Describe how the satellite image tells you about the kind of weather to expect?

2 Take special note of the weather the next day.

   a) Write down details of the weather, including taking some measurements.

   b) Describe how the weather has changed during the day.

   c) How accurate has the forecast been?

3 Check the weather pattern then make your own predictions for the next day.
   See how accurate your forecast has been.

Sample activity; study skills

1   Choose one or more of the topics that is on your GCSE examination syllabus.

   a) Find the BBC website (http://www.bbc.co.uk/education/cdb/index.shtml) that helps with GCSE revision.
Choose the section that gives help with geography (http://db.bbc.co.uk/education-bitesize/pkg_main.p_topics?in_id=125).

   b) Work through the learning program to revise the basic ideas about the topic.
Open a word processor document and transfer useful items into it.

   c) Beside each key idea, write down your own reminders about the case studies you have studied in your own geography lessons.

2   Check that you have learnt the key words and ideas.

   a) Do this by by working through the test section on the BBC web site.

   b) If you want further details about your case studies or want additional case studies, use the Internet search engines to see what you can find or access a web site that you already know may be of use.
Remember however, that it may not be a good idea to either learning new case study material, or spending time finding it.

Index